Praise for *Pagan Threat*

"A fearless warrior for Christ. Lucas is a man built to stand for the truth in a time of great apostasy. Don't just read *Pagan Threat*—internalize what it has to say. Then, share its message with your Christian friends, before they are seduced by Paganism themselves. We have a faith and a country to save."

　　—**CHARLIE KIRK**, founder and president of Turning Point USA, host of *The Charlie Kirk Show*, and *New York Times* bestselling author of *The MAGA Doctrine*

"In *Pagan Threat*, Lucas Miles prophetically exposes the spiritual forces at work beneath our culture's rapid moral decline. With biblical clarity and pastoral urgency, he calls the church to wake up, stand firm, and re-engage the culture with the truth of the Gospel. This is a timely and sobering read for every believer who desires to be faithful in an increasingly hostile age."

　　—**ROBERT PACIENZA**, Senior Pastor of Coral Ridge Presbyterian Church

"In his new book, *Pagan Threat*, Lucas Miles doesn't just highlight the rise of witchcraft and demonic influence in America—he calls for a bold spiritual counteroffensive. This book urgently reminds Christians that the fight is not just cultural but spiritual, as we face a growing darkness that seeks to dismantle everything we hold dear. If we are to reclaim the future of our nation and our faith, it's time to start standing firm in the truth."

　　—**ALLEN JACKSON**, Senior Pastor of World Outreach Church

"Lucas Miles has written a powerful and urgent book that every believer needs to read. *Pagan Threat* isn't just about the rise of paganism—it's about the call to action for the Church to unite, stand firm in biblical doctrine, and fight for the soul of our nation. This book challenges us to set aside our differences and unite around the essential truths of the Gospel—before it's too late. It's a bold invitation for Christians to rise above the cultural chaos and take our rightful place in advancing the Kingdom of God."

—JENTEZEN FRANKLIN, Senior Pastor of Free Chapel, and *New York Times* bestselling author of *Fasting*

"Over the years, I've worked with more than 1,000 pastors and ministry leaders, and I can confidently say that Lucas Miles has become one of our most significant leaders in engaging the culture with the Gospel. He's spent years researching and understanding what's influencing this generation, and is unafraid to take a message of hope to the darkest places. His new book, *Pagan Threat: Confronting America's Godless Uprising*, has become my playbook for understanding and responding to today's rising tide of paganism. Get the book. Teach it to your congregation. Help prepare them for the threats coming after Christian families today. We're farther down that road than we think."

—PHIL COOKE, PhD, filmmaker, media consultant, and author of *Church on Trial: How to Protect Your Congregation, Mission, and Reputation During a Crisis*

"Bold, clear, and unafraid—*Pagan Threat* gives believers the insight and tools we need to stand firm in truth."

—KEVIN SORBO, actor, director, and bestselling author of *True Strength*

"Lucas Miles has a way of peeling back the layers of our cultural confusion to reveal what's really going on beneath the surface. *Pagan Threat* is both a wake-up call and a roadmap for anyone who's felt the ground shifting beneath their feet. It's honest, direct, and refreshingly grounded."

—EDGAR STRUBLE, producer of *The Heart Mender*,
music director, Academy of Country Music Awards

"The good news is that America is becoming more spiritual. The bad news is that the unbiblical pursuit of spirituality is leading a whole generation toward disaster. The old 'New Age' movement has come roaring back and it's much more diverse and sophisticated—ensnaring many Christians. This book powerfully explains what is going on and how to stand strong even as the rising tide of paganism threatens to engulf us."

—JEFF MYERS, PhD, president of Summit Ministries

"Lucas Miles is not just a friend but a passionate advocate for truth in a world where many shy away from difficult conversations. In his new book, *Pagan Threat: Confronting America's Godless Uprising*, he tackles the pressing issues facing Christianity today, addressing the paganistic ideologies that threaten our youth. This may very well be Lucas's finest work, as he provides the church with biblical answers that are both relevant and necessary."

—JASON JIMENEZ, president of Stand Strong Ministries,
respected Christian apologist, bestselling author of
Challenging Conversations and *Hijacking Jesus: How
Progressives Are Remaking Him and Taking Over His
Church*

"Another brilliant book by Lucas Miles! How tragically ironic when, in pursuit of intimacy, we could reject the lover of our souls. In pursuit of secret knowledge, we could reject the knowledge of the glory of God in the face of Christ Jesus. In pursuit of power, we reject the life-giving power of the risen God. In pursuit of spirituality, we reject the Holy Spirit who breathes joy into our otherwise lost lives.

This book is a prayer—revive us, again!"

—KELLY MONROE KULLBERG, author, *Finding God at Harvard*, founder of the Veritas Forum, General Secretary, American Association of Evangelicals (AAE)

PAGAN THREAT

CONFRONTING AMERICA'S GODLESS UPRISING

LUCAS MILES

Humanix Books

www.humanixbooks.com

Humanix Books
Pagan Threat: Confronting America's Godless Uprising
Copyright © 2025 by Lucas Miles

Cover design by Bijou McMillion, NovaEthica

ISBN: 978-163006-292-7 (Hardcover)
ISBN: 978-163006-293-4 (E-book)

Printed in the United States of America
10 9 8 7 6

To the faithful—those who refuse to bow to Baal.

Contents

Foreword

"There is nothing new under the sun," Solomon wrote in the Book of Ecclesiastes. What is experienced today has been experienced before. What has happened in the past will happen again.

That's good to know. Because in today's America, the Christian faithful are faced with a terrifying and broad array of dangers and threats. It is good to know that there's nothing unique about these evils. Every one of them has a precedent. We are menaced not by new false gods, but by the return of demons from long ago.

To those raised in a Christian world, it's easy to take its moral innovations for granted. Even atheists benefit from living in the world that Christians made. And the surest sign that we are living in an evil modern age is that the forces of modernity are fanatically fighting to restore the moral order that existed prior to Christianity: In other words, the moral order of the Pagans.

In the Pagan world, the individual human life was of no importance. Therefore abortion, infanticide, human sacrifice, and more were just a part of life. Under Paganism, there was no notion that humans had equal innate worth, so one tribe enslaved another, or rulers enslaved their subjects, all with impunity.

I've been friends with Lucas for some time now. I've come to know him as a speaker, pastor, and partner at Turning Point USA Faith. But above all, I know him as a fearless warrior for Christ. Lucas is a man built to stand for the truth in a time of great apostasy. And the era we live in is a time of apostasy that would make the Old Testament prophets shudder.

The revival of those Old Testament times is exactly what this book, *Pagan Threat: Confronting America's Godless Uprising*, confronts. Casual Christians like to imagine we have already won a permanent victory over the worshipers of Moloch, Baal, and Jupiter, but those gods are now back with a vengeance bearing new names like "progressivism," "tolerance," and "social justice." This new Paganism says a lot about "freedom," but just like the old Pagans, its ultimate agenda is domination and moral anarchy. Christians seduced by its superficial words will find themselves betrayed—or making an alliance with the devil.

Thankfully, people like Lucas have realized the danger and are fighting back. They are fighting back with a true vision of Christianity—one that isn't always polite and isn't always "nice," but *is* always on fire for the Lord and His truth.

This book will not always be comfortable to read. It's not pleasant to realize that our faith and our way of life are in danger. Denial is always more pleasant in the moment. But if you are willing to open its pages with a heart tuned to the Holy Spirit, it will also equip you and embolden you to see clearly, speak truthfully, and stand firmly in the face of darkness.

Don't just read this book—internalize what it has to say. Then, share its message with your Christian friends, before they are seduced by Paganism themselves. We have a faith and a country to save.

Charlie Kirk

Introduction

In my last two books, I warned of the deceptive infiltration of Woke thought that has broken through the defensive walls of the church, quickly cloaking itself with orthodox appearances to remain relatively unnoticed. That is, until recently, when the true nature of this ideology began to reveal itself with alarming clarity. The encroachment of Woke ideology was just the precursor to a more profound and unsettling threat: the resurgence of Paganism.

The seemingly innocuous rise of social justice and inclusivity movements has laid the groundwork for a full-blown revival of ancient Pagan beliefs. What initially appeared as a benign cultural trend is a deliberate and dark movement towards a reawakening of occult practices and ideologies, which, at their core, are inherently anti-Christian. This book, *Pagan Threat: Confronting America's Godless Uprising*, aims to shed light on how the ancient and the modern have converged in ways that threaten both the church and the broader fabric of our society.

The connection between Woke ideology and Paganism is not merely a coincidence but a natural progression. Behind the emphasis on identity politics, intersectionality, and radical inclusivity within Wokeism lies centuries-old ancient Pagan ideologies.

As such, it could be stated that Wokeism is not new, but rather the modern fruition of ancient Paganism. What has appeared political and secular, is spiritual.

This, of course, explains the zeal with which Wokeism is promoted. Just as the Pagans of old were devoted to their gods and rituals, today's Woke adherents are fervent in their devotion to the new dogmas of gender identity, Critical Race Theory, and Earth worship. It is a religion in all but name, with its own sacred texts, high priests, and rituals of penance and purification.

In this emerging neo-Pagan cult, culture serves as a form of negative evangelism, demonstrating the consequences of failing to adhere to the Left's playbook. What might appear as coerced ideological or political agreement is a type of forced spiritual conversion. Acting as a modern-day inquisition, cancel culture imposes these conversions through public shaming, deplatforming, and societal ostracization. Those who refuse to bow to the idols of this neo-Paganistic worldview are excommunicated from the public square, much like heretics of old were cast out from their communities. The zeal with which this ideology is enforced reveals its true nature—not merely as a political movement but as a spiritual influence seeking to force itself on the very soul of society.

Aligning together in this effort are Marxists, radical environmentalists, technocratic scientists, LGBTQ+ activists, so-called racial justice activists, eugenicists, witches, traditional Pagans, neo-Pagans, and theosophical elites. Together, they have infiltrated major nonprofit organizations, entertainment agencies and studios, research labs, religious institutions, educational centers, and countless government agencies. Through this collective influence, they have successfully transformed the global spiritual consciousness away from Christianity toward a neo-Pagan resurgence.

In this new world, Christian values have been reduced to archaic bigotry, as the new ethic of the religious Left establishes itself as the preferred zeitgeist of the reimagined global order. An order where abortion, gender reassignment surgery, and gain-of-function research are offered as sacraments to a modern pantheon made up of deities like Gaia and Isis, along with the apotheosis of a global state and even humanity itself. This emerging ideology elevates these elements to divine status, transforming political and social policies into sacred rites, and reshaping the very essence of moral and spiritual discourse.

Quite frankly, the church wasn't ready for this. Working under the assumption that Paganism was dead, Christians failed to take seriously the incremental reawakening of false ideology and heretical ideas that was taking place before our eyes, and at times, even under our steeples. Through the introduction of the Enneagram, the acceptance of immoral sexual practices, the embrace of New Age concepts such as energy healing and visualization exercises that blur the lines between Christian faith and occult practices, the promotion of Christian universalism, astral projection, and sage cleansing rituals, the church has been quietly flooded with pseudo-Christian Pagan ideologies that threaten the orthodox foundations of Christianity in America.

This blurring of Christian and cultic, combined with a diminished interest in "organized religion," due, at least in part, to the recent wave of pastoral impropriety in which multiple nationally recognized pastors like Carl Lentz, Ravi Zacharias, Tony Evans, and Robert Morris faced accusations and scandals during their time in the pulpit and left behind a wake of spiritual and emotional carnage. Pouring gas on the growing flames of ministerial distrust is a long line of deconstructionist-oriented online influencers, like Dan McClellan, Brenda Marie Davies, and Brandon Robertson, who make their living either steering people away from the faith or toward more progressive variations of it.

Common to these individuals are an eroded view of Scripture, a progressive sexual ethic, and a strong critique of historical Christian beliefs, which for many nominal believers is enough to shipwreck their faith. Their deconstructionist approach often involves dismantling the authority of Scripture, recasting it as a flawed human document rather than the divinely inspired Word of God. By doing so, they strip away the Bible's moral and theological absolutes, replacing them with a more fluid and subjective interpretation that aligns with modern cultural trends. This reinterpretation often downplays, or outright rejects, traditional Christian teachings on issues like sexuality, marriage, and the sanctity of life, promoting instead a theology that is more palatable to contemporary sensibilities, but is fundamentally at odds with biblical Christianity.

These influencers leverage social media platforms to reach millions, disseminating their revisionist ideas with a persuasive mix of charisma, emotional appeal, and intellectual critique. Their teachings resonate particularly with younger generations, who may already feel disconnected from traditional church structures and seek a more inclusive and affirming spiritual path. However, the result is a form of Christianity that bears little resemblance to its historical roots, or worse yet, an abandonment of the faith altogether into more Pagan elements such as pantheism, goddess worship, and modern forms of witchcraft.

This trend is deeply troubling, not just because it leads individuals away from the truth of the Gospel, but because it weakens the church's ability to stand as a countercultural witness in an increasingly Pagan society. When the church loses its distinctiveness—when it begins to mirror the values and beliefs of the surrounding culture rather than challenge them—it ceases to be the transformative force it was meant to be. Instead, it becomes just another voice in the chorus of competing worldviews, offering little more than spiritualized self-help and moralistic platitudes.

This, of course, is exactly what's happened. For the first time since the days of the Roman Empire, Christians are being accused of holding views that are not only out of step with contemporary values but are deemed actively harmful to societal progress. Where past criticisms of Christianity may have labeled believers as "holier-than-thou" or "outdated," today's charges are far more severe. Christians are now branded as barriers to justice, as purveyors of harm, and even as threats to inclusivity and collective advancement. The church is portrayed as a dam to progress rather than a wellspring of hope and truth.

This shift in perception reflects a wider cultural transformation where traditional Christian teachings are not only dismissed but actively opposed. The church's core doctrines are increasingly viewed as obstacles to societal advancement rather than as sources of moral and spiritual guidance. In this environment, the church's role as a moral compass is under siege, and its voice is increasingly marginalized in public discourse.

Ultimately, if this trend continues, Christian persecution in America and other Western nations seems inevitable. The erosion of religious freedoms, the criminalization of traditional beliefs, and the societal rejection of core Christian values are not distant possibilities but present realities. As the cultural frontlines grow more hostile, Christians must brace themselves for escalating tensions and increasing opposition—politically and spiritually.

To navigate this challenging era, Christians must renew their commitment to biblical truth while engaging the culture with grace and conviction. A new apologetic is needed—one that not only defends the faith but also actively reclaims the moral and spiritual authority of Christianity in the public square. This means addressing contemporary issues (which many pastors are currently unwilling or unable to tackle) with a thoughtful and biblical response that bridges the gap between the ancient truths of the Gospel and the pressing needs of modern society.

A true third Great Awakening, characterized by a widespread return to heartfelt faith and transformative revival, could also counteract this growing tide. Such an awakening would not only rejuvenate the church but restore its role as a beacon of hope and moral clarity. Until that transformative shift occurs, Christians must prepare for a period of intense scrutiny and opposition and stand firm in their convictions while seeking to embody the love, justice, and truth of Christ in an increasingly secular world.

It cannot be forgotten that any successful spiritual defense against a modern Pagan resurgence must also include the active presence and welcomed operation of the Holy Spirit. As we face an era of unprecedented spiritual conflict, the Holy Spirit remains our guide, comforter, and source of divine power, equipping us to both proclaim and demonstrate our witness. Embracing the Holy Spirit's work in our lives and the church will be crucial to reclaiming the narrative and advancing God's Kingdom in these trying times.

Furthermore, we must cultivate a deep and vibrant spiritual life that goes beyond mere church attendance, intellectual assent, and doctrinal statements. We need a renewal of genuine Christian discipleship, where believers are not only taught the truths of the faith but are also formed in the likeness of Christ through the practices of prayer, worship, and intimacy with God. Only by embodying the Gospel in this way can we hope to withstand the onslaught of Pagan ideologies and be a light in dark places.

Finally, we must be vigilant in guarding our churches from the infiltration of these false teachings. This means being discerning about the books we read, the speakers we listen to, and the movements we align ourselves with. It also means having the courage to confront error when we see it, whether it comes from a popular preacher, a well-intentioned friend, or our own hearts. The stakes are too high for us to be complacent. The future of the church—and indeed, the soul of our nation—depends on our willingness to stand firm in the faith once delivered to the saints.

It is with this spirit that this book does more than diagnose the threats we face; it aims to equip and inspire us to rise to the challenge. As we journey into the chapters ahead, we will explore the intricate ways in which neo-Pagan ideologies are infiltrating both the church and the broader culture. We will examine the theological, cultural, and practical aspects of the resurgence and uncover strategies for countering these threats with biblical truth and spiritual vitality.

By understanding the nature of the Pagan threat and the ways it manifests, we can better prepare ourselves to engage with the world from a place of deep, Spirit-filled conviction. We will uncover how the early church stood firm amidst persecution and apply these lessons to our current context. Through prayerful reflection, renewed commitment to discipleship, and vigilant discernment, we can reclaim the narrative and strengthen our witness in a culture increasingly hostile to the Gospel.

In the pages that follow, I invite you to embark on this adventure of spiritual awakening. Together, let us seek the guidance of the Holy Spirit, embrace the transformative power of revival, and stand resolute against the encroaching darkness. The future of the church and our great nation depends on our collective faithfulness to the truth and our unwavering commitment to the Kingdom of God.

ONE

A NEW PAGAN GENERATION

THE RISE OF THE OTHER RELIGIONS

A delicate white linen toga, held fast by a gold-colored thread, clings to a young woman's frame as she immerses herself in a rite of purification before casting an ancient goêteia spell.[1] Her arms are intricately tattooed, and a gold ring hangs from her nose. While this scene may sound like the start of a Hellenistic tale from antiquity, it isn't. The woman, who goes by "Thorn," is a TikTok influencer with a quarter of a million followers who refers to herself as a "sorcerer" and a "man-hating Satanic lesbian."[2]

Not alone, Thorn is part of a rapidly growing subset of the American population who have rejected Abrahamic faiths, such as Christianity and Judaism, in favor of "other religions," broadly being described as "Pagan." Thorn's demographic, which has already expanded to over 1.5 million Americans, is expected to triple by 2050.[3] Making up a large portion of these new Pagan converts are Millennials and Gen Zers (Zoomers), who are trading cross necklaces, Bible studies, and youth groups for crystals, tarot cards, and seances.

Collectively known as the "Harry Potter Generation,"[4] Millennials and Zoomers, who grew up with dreams of attending Hogwarts, playing Dungeons & Dragons, or forming friendships through LARPing (live action role-playing), are no strangers to

3

wizardry and witchcraft. However, an affinity for fantasy isn't the sole factor driving their departure from traditional faiths. Their shared experiences of traumatic events also play a role. Chief among these are September 11, 2001, the alarming increase in school shootings,[5] and the isolation and distrust stemming from the COVID-19 shutdown,[6] all contributing to Millennials' and Zoomers' inclination toward exploring and experimenting with alternative religious practices.

Additionally, fueling the significant growth in American Paganism, especially among the next generation, are websites like Outschool.com, which boasts more than ten interactive "Online Witchcraft Classes for Teens,"[7] as well as, WiccaAcademy.com, which offers courses in "tarot card readings," "spellcrafting," and "basic magick"[8] advertised to help you "become the witch who you were meant to be."[9] Further galvanizing the interest in Pagan revival are celebrities like supermodel Gisele Bündchen, who was reported to use "an altar," "healing stones," and "mantras" to help her former husband and NFL great Tom Brady win seven Super Bowl victories,[10] and pop icon Lana del Rey, who "urged her fans to take part in a group hexing of President Donald Trump" for three consecutive months "in alignment with the waning moon."[11]

Backing up these celebrities is Hollywood which, has been complicit for years in introducing Pagan practices to America's youth. From seemingly innocuous animated films, like Disney's *The Little Mermaid* and *Frozen*, to edgier Netflix' teen-focused original series, like *The Order* and *Chilling Adventures of Sabrina*, Tinseltown has displayed no restraint in producing programs glorifying Pagan practices such as rituals and ceremonies, magic, witchcraft, nature worship, deity worship, indigenous traditions, and shamanism. More than just revolting against biblical faith, many of these programs also intertwine other anti-establishment and deconstructive themes, such as feminist subculture, queer theory, and pro-Marxist ideology,[12] dismantling the younger generations' belief in God, while simultaneously grooming them into radical critical activists.

But despite the ubiquity of this neo-Pagan movement and the real threat it poses to the American way of life, many people (especially those in the church) seem to lack a useful definition of Pagan practices and fail to realize the massive ways in which Paganism is transforming culture right before their eyes. If we are to confront this spiritual adversary and win over an expanding Pagan generation for Christ, then we must first "demolish arguments and every proud thing that is raised up against the knowledge of God" and "take every thought captive to obey Christ."[13] But to do so, we must first understand what we are up against.

PAGANISM DEFINED

Once considered obsolete, "Paganism" is a blanket term used to describe those who have abandoned mainstream forms of religion for esoteric practices, often rooted in polytheism, ancient rituals, worship of nature, spell-casting, sexual acts, and altered states of consciousness (with or without psychedelic substances). Falling under the broad terminology of "Pagan" exists a virtually endless and ever-expanding list of self-identifications, such as Wicca, druidism, occult, Heathenism, witchcraft, Neo-Pagan, Shamanism, Thelema, Theosophy, New Age, New Thought, Baltic, Celtic, Hellenistic, Norse Reconstructionism, eclectic Paganism, and more. Dividing even further, each of these categories is broken down into countless versions and personal expressions, making modern Paganism the ultimate deconstructive practice for personal self-expression.

As we will see, the various forms of Paganism resurrecting in America's religious landscape today are simply ritualistic fingers of a much broader and more complex religious parent cult, which has been lurking in the shadows of modern Woke culture, quietly guiding the social justice activists, gender warriors, and globalist elites for over a century. But before we fully expose what all the various forms of Paganism have in common and the sinister esoteric beliefs driving their rise to power, it's important that we first examine them individually.

TYPES OF MODERN PAGANISM

While by no means exhaustive, here is a brief list of the primary Pagan practices seeing a resurgence in America today:

Druidism

Primarily a modern invention, neo-Druidism emerged at the end of the eighteenth-century Romantic Era from renewed interest in Celtic culture and spirituality. Today, Druid practitioners seek to reimagine, albeit with limited historical and archaeological evidence, the religious paths and rituals of the ancient Druid priestly class, with an added emphasis on nature, cycles of the seasons, and the sacredness of the land.

Wicca

Wicca is a modern Pagan religious movement that emerged in the mid-twentieth century, drawing upon ancient Pagan and esoteric traditions. It emphasizes reverence for nature, worship of the divine in both feminine and masculine forms (often referred to as the Goddess and the God), and the practice of magic. Wiccans typically celebrate seasonal festivals, known as Sabbats, and conduct rituals that involve casting circles, invoking deities, and spellcraft.

Heathenism

Modern Heathenism, also known as contemporary Heathenry or Heathenry Revivalism, refers to a modern Pagan religious movement that seeks to revive and reconstruct the religious beliefs, practices, and cultural traditions of the ancient Germanic peoples, particularly those of pre-Christian Northern Europe. It encompasses a diverse range of polytheistic beliefs and practices, drawing inspiration from historical sources such as mythology, sagas, folklore, and archaeological findings. Practitioners of Modern Heathenism often engage in rituals, ceremonies, and seasonal celebrations inspired by historical practices, as well as personal devotional practices and ancestor veneration that emphasize cultural heritage, folk traditions, and a deep connection to the land and natural world.

Thelema

Thelema (*they-LEE-mah*) is a blended spiritual and philosophical system developed by Aleister Crowley in the early twentieth century, rooted in his personal study of hermeticism, eastern mysticism, and ceremonial magic. The term "Thelema" is derived from the Greek word for *will* or *desire*, and the central tenet of Thelema is "Do what thou wilt shall be the whole of the Law," commonly shortened to "Do what thou wilt." Key practices in Thelema include ceremonial magic, meditation, yoga, and ritual work. Crowley developed a system of magical practices and rituals, known as "Thelemic magick," which are designed to help practitioners awaken their true will, attain spiritual enlightenment, and commune with higher spirit guides or entities known as "Holy Guardian Angels."[14] Central to Crowley's teachings are a belief in the inherent divinity of every individual and the idea that each person has the potential to achieve spiritual liberation and self-realization.

Shamanism

Shamanism is a spiritual and cultural practice found in various indigenous societies around the world. Shamanic practices typically involve rituals, ceremonies, and journeys into altered states of consciousness induced through techniques such as drumming, chanting, dancing, or the use of psychoactive substances. During these journeys, shamans claim encounters with spirits, ancestors, or animal guides, seeking guidance, healing powers, or insight for themselves or others.

Witchcraft

Witchcraft is a multifaceted spiritual and magical practice that encompasses a wide range of beliefs, rituals, and traditions. At its core, witchcraft involves the harnessing and manipulation of natural energies to effect change in the physical world or in oneself. Practitioners of witchcraft, known as "witches," may draw upon various sources such as folklore, mythology, herbalism, astrology, dark magic, and divination to deepen their understanding and enhance their magical workings.

Occultism

The term "occult" comes from the Latin word *occultus*, meaning "hidden" or "secret."[15] Through the practice of magic, mysticism, alchemy, astrology, divination, and spiritualism, occultists seek to uncover hidden truths about the nature of reality, the universe, and the human experience through various means, often involving rituals, symbolism, and the exploration of altered states of consciousness. Historically, occultism has been associated with mystery schools, secret societies, and esoteric traditions dating back to ancient times. However, it experienced a resurgence in the late Middle Ages and Renaissance periods with the revival of Hermeticism, alchemy, and Kabbalah.

Secular Paganism

Secular Paganism involves engaging with Pagan traditions and folklore from a cultural or philosophical perspective, without necessarily incorporating belief in supernatural beings or deities. Secular Paganism offers a way to engage with Pagan heritage and practices while maintaining a more atheistic or agnostic religious framework.

Theosophy

Theosophy is an esoteric spiritual and philosophical movement that emerged in the late nineteenth century, founded by Helena Petrovna Blavatsky, Henry Steel Olcott, and others. The term "Theosophy" is derived from the Greek words *theos* (god) and *sophia* (wisdom) and carries with it the meaning of divine wisdom or knowledge of the divine. Central themes within Theosophy include the unity of all existence, the interconnectedness of all life forms, the doctrine of karma (the law of cause and effect), reincarnation, the idea of spiritual evolution and self-transformation, and the existence of a spiritual hierarchy of enlightened beings who guide human evolution. The Theosophical Society, founded in 1875,[16] serves as a central organization for the dissemination of Theosophical teachings and the exploration of spiritual and philosophical ideas.

New Age

New Age religion refers to a broad and eclectic spiritual movement that emerged in the latter half of the twentieth century, characterized by an emphasis on personal growth, holistic healing, and the exploration of metaphysical and esoteric concepts. New Age practitioners often engage in practices such as meditation, yoga, energy or crystal healing, astrology, and channeling, seeking to align with higher consciousness and tap into inner wisdom. Central to New Age spirituality is the belief in the existence of a universal energy or life force that permeates the cosmos, often referred to as "Spirit," "Source," or "the Divine." While New Age religion is diverse and decentralized, with no central authority or dogma, it has had a significant influence on contemporary spirituality, wellness, and popular culture.

New Thought

New Thought emerged primarily in the nineteenth-century United States and is based on the teachings of figures like Phineas Quimby and Mary Baker Eddy. It emphasizes the power of positive thinking, the creative power of the mind, and the use of spiritual practices such as visualization and affirmation to improve one's life and well-being. New Thought often has a more explicitly Christian orientation, although it incorporates elements from various religious and philosophical traditions.

Baltic, Celtic, Hellenistic, or Norse Reconstructionism

Baltic, Celtic, Hellenistic, and Norse Paganism are geographic poly-theistic religious reconstructions rooted in the historical practices of ancient people groups and the various pantheons they vener-ated. Each of these traditions seeks to revive the spiritual customs, deities, and cultural heritage of their respective regions, drawing from archaeological findings, historical texts, and mythology to reconstruct religious rituals and beliefs. For instance, Hellenistic Reconstructionists study the philosophical and religious tra-ditions of ancient Greece, celebrating the Olympian gods and engaging in rites inspired by ancient Greek rituals, while Norse Reconstructionists revere the Norse pantheon, including gods like Odin, Thor, and Freyja, through ceremonies and practices assem-bled by historical sources.

Eclectic Paganism

Eclectic Paganism is a "choose-your-own-adventure" spiritual approach that draws from various Pagan traditions, beliefs, and practices, creating a personalized and syncretic path tailored to individual preferences and spiritual needs. For example, an Eclectic Pagan may worship a Norse deity, cast Wiccan spells, and reconnect with nature through Druidry, all without any need to verify or validate their unique practice through history or ancient religious texts.

Everything Is Sacred

Detached from the precepts of traditional faith, modern Pagans, no matter their identification, redefine Judeo-Christian morality as they seek to reconnect with the "ancient ways." Senior editor at

The Federalist and author of *Pagan America* John Daniel Davidson explains that this redefinition of morality allows Pagans to see truth as "relative," leaving practitioners "free to ascribe sacred or divine status to the here and now, to things or activities, even to human beings"[17] as they see fit. According to Davidson, this grants Pagans "a moral relativism in which power alone determines right."[18]

This is exactly what Planned Parenthood contributor Rae Guerra-Lorenzo displayed when she leaned into her indigenous Pagan roots and declared, "Abortion is sacred. And the Supreme Court can't take that away from us."[19] Guerra-Lorenzo, who uses "they/them" pronouns and describes herself as a "Mescalero Apache/Laguna Pueblo/Xicana" and "a queer parent of two," is the co-founder of Indigenous Women Rising, which among other activities, promotes abortion rights for Indigenous women. Stating her case, Guerra-Lorenzo adds:

> *Yes, our children in this realm are sacred. They are sacred because they are the entities into which we pour our time and love because we want to, not because we are forced to. No one should be forced to stay pregnant if they don't want to. I am here because of abortion—someone down the line of ancestors knew when it was and wasn't time for expanding their family. My own children are here because of abortion. Just as my children and yours are sacred, so is our decision to have an abortion.*

Children aren't sacred to Guerra-Lorenzo, because, without biblical values like the sanctity of life, no human being is made in the image of God. Rather, humans only have value because she, and others like her, have ascribed value to them. According to her indigenous beliefs, when lives aren't valued, they are easily disposed of through abortion. And, conveniently, thanks to her moral relativism, abortion in turn becomes sacred because she believes that any opposition to her beliefs is oppressive. In this way, "sanctity" provides protection for moral relativism, and questionable actions, beliefs, or practices, like abortion, are ascribed value.

This is further illustrated by an article entitled "Sacred Bodies," from Harvard University's *The Pluralism Project*, which confesses:

> . . . *the feminist movement begins with lived experience and affirms that "the personal is political." In feminist Paganism, the personal and political are also spiritual. Many women are drawn to the way Paganism helps them put spiritual ideals into practice and how Goddess imagery in particular can be used for both spiritual and social liberation.*[20]

Perhaps more candidly than Guerra-Lorenzo, *The Pluralism Project* admits that within the realm of Paganism, not only personal beliefs and ethics but also political positions and agendas, are allowed under the sacred or "spiritual" canopy, often invoked in the pursuit of social liberation. For those unacquainted with the term, "social liberation" serves as a coded language among critical theorists, signifying aspirations toward a "socialist revolution."

This insight reveals the genuine utility of Paganism—to act as a carrier oil for the Woke parasitical virus of Marxist ideology. As I wrote in my previous work, *The Christian Left: How Liberal Thought has Hijacked the Church*, this same tactic was used to insert Woke thought into Christianity:

> *Much like the infamous tactical device of the Ancient Greeks, the devil has "gifted" our modern-day society with Trojan horses too: ideologies that appear to be valuable*

*contributions to our faith but are instead full of morally
subversive stratagems designed to unravel the very
theological framework of the church. Slipping past the walls
of Christian orthodoxy and sound doctrine, this barrage of
intellectual and spiritual attacks has produced what is now
being called "the Christian Left"—a growing constituency
of "Christians" who have adopted (either knowingly or
unknowingly) leftist, socialist, and communistic thinking,
ideals, values, and innovations.*[21]

While it's apparent that Wokeism has successfully infiltrated major swaths of the American church, as evidenced by continued denominational turmoil exhibited in groups like the United Methodist Church and the Southern Baptist Convention, most have failed to recognize that the virus' tenure within the four walls of Christian orthodoxy is ultimately self-limiting. By nature, Christianity, while an excellent short-term distribution system for ideological thought, is a poor long-term host for heretical ideas. The reason for this, which is often overlooked, is that Christianity itself maintains a robust internal rigidity allowing it to retain its doctrinal formation in resistance to both external and internal pressures. More specifically, key scriptural ideas protect the Christian faith and help to reset it back to the center (what we call "orthodoxy") every time false notions are presented. A few of these protective beliefs are:

- The unchanging nature of God and His Word (*see* Psalm 102:27, Psalm 119:89, Malachi 3:6, James 1:17)
- Salvation by grace through faith (*see* Ephesians 2:8-9, Titus 3:5, Romans 3:28)
- The supremacy of the Lord Jesus Christ (*see* Hebrews 1:3, Philippians 2:9-11, Colossians 1:15-20)

- The authority of the Word of God (*see* 2 Timothy 3:16-17, Matthew 4:4, 2 Peter 1:20-21)
- The depravity of man (*see* Romans 3:10-12, Jeremiah 17:9, Romans 3:23)

Though some might attempt to overlook or redefine primary Christian truths such as these, any serious study of the faith inevitably requires revisiting original source material (that is, the Holy Bible) to gain additional spiritual understanding and theological mastery. When this takes place (at least with any sort of academic honesty) one of two things will happen: One's faith will be discarded for more strongly held progressive views (i.e., marriage or sexuality), or the progressive views themselves will be exposed as contradictory to pure Christian faith and rejected in submission to Christ. Bluntly stated, either the host dies, or the parasite is exposed.

In the church, Wokeism's days are numbered, as the more you push into the biblical text, the more Marxist and Woke ideology are self-refuted.

Unfortunately, the same is not so with Paganism. Lacking the structural integrity of Christian orthodoxy and a fixed understanding of absolute truth, Paganism is a much more suitable and beneficial long-term environment for the Woke parasite to take root. With its diverse, varied history, limited historical texts, and oftentimes egregious moral relativism, Paganism warmly welcomes Woke thought, such as gender ideology and Critical Race Theory, without complaint. For practices that once incorporated human sacrifice[22] and still espouse polyamorous sexual relationships,[23] it's hardly a stretch to think that Paganism would find kindredness with the Marxist view of class struggle, especially when viewed through the dialectical synthesis of the sacred on one side and oppressive on the other. This mystical union between critical consciousness and unfettered spiritual enlightenment allows Pagans to find strategic allies among other activist subcultures more than Progressive Christianity ever could.

WITCHCRAFT: THE NEW MARXIST PRAXIS

"It is well known that Paganism and witchcraft have been pushed to the sidelines and marginalized since Christianity began its stronghold. So has queerness,"[24] writes Cassandra Snow, author of *Queering Your Craft: Witchcraft from the Margins*.

For Snow, who teaches "tarot from a radically queer and intersectional perspective,"[25] Paganism and progressivist activism go together and join in rebellion against the ultimate oppressor: Christianity. Snow's solution is simple: "If we are to be witches, with a duty to humankind and the Earth itself, and to serve social justice, we cannot always be polite and harm-free."[26] Continuing she adds, "In a politically difficult and tense world, witchcraft is a secret weapon."[27] More than just a figure of speech, Snow's book provides her readers with a framework of specific hexes and spells to utilize her "secret weapon" of witchcraft, such as:

- A Spell to Slow Down the Effects of Climate Change[28]
- A Spell to Protect Our Community from Legislative Harm[29]
- A Spell to Attract Sex Partners[30]
- Hexing the White Supremacist Patriarchy[31]
- A Spell for Comfort Over Religious Trauma Syndrome[32]
- A Spell to Protect Activists[33]
- A Spell of Protection Against the Patriarchy[34]
- A Hex on Those Who Rail Against Queer Rights[35]

Embedded within Snow's critical theory-inspired prescriptions for spellcraft is what Brazilian critical pedagogue Paulo Freire, termed *conscientização*, or a higher critical consciousness. Freire, a hero for many modern Woke warriors like Snow, used his new educational theory, known as Critical Pedagogy, for the purpose of radicalizing learners and grooming future activists for societal liberation.

Political commentator and a leading critic of Marxist thought, Dr. James Lindsay, who rightly refers to Freire's ideas, like those proposed by Snow, as a "crackpot theory of education,"[36] explains that Critical Pedagogy is to blame for "failing to teach our children basic skills like reading, writing, and mathematics"[37] while simultaneously "succeeding at turning them into a new activist class for Leftist—and only and explicitly Leftist—causes."[38] According to Lindsay, this radicalization is no accident and "is what Freire's educational theory is designed to achieve. Students are meant to be 'facilitated' into Leftist political activism, and other student achievement outcomes are quite literally an afterthought. Education is a pretext; Marxist activist grooming is the point."[39]

For Freire's Critical Pedagogy to be effective in a widely Christian nation, Christianity must first be subverted. Exposing Freire's intentions, Dr. Lindsay writes:

Freire, then, is literally calling the existing society and Christian church a death cult and any functional educational system within it a mode of maintaining and reproducing that evil. His answer is equally religious: calling to remake education and the churches entirely as an opposing form of religious education into political consciousness "on the side of the oppressed." To accomplish this, he specifically calls upon educators to die to the existing order of society and resurrect themselves as people with (Marxist) consciousness.[40]

The foremost "existing order" that these educators, specifically critical pedagogues, must "die to" is Christian thought. While heretical forms of the Christian faith, such as Progressive Christianity and Liberation Theology—both significantly influenced by Freire's writings—provided a short-term subversion of the existing religious order, they fell short of completely dismantling the Christian influence in America. Eventually, a new religious antithesis would be required, one that could act as a more attractive replacement for the Christian faith and serve as a better ally for Marxist ideology.

Pagan and occult traditions are more aptly suited for this new role and are now entwined with Marxist ideology to liberate us from the prevailing moral constraints and theological narrow-mindedness of orthodox thought. This happy marriage has presented a pathway for putting to rest the existing order—a predominantly Christian America—and ushering in a "rebirth" of a post-Christian society. For modern occultists like Snow, this new alliance between Paganism and Marxism produced a newfound critical consciousness, transforming their worship from mere ritual to revolution. Driven by the adoption of praxis, defined by Freire as "the reflection and action which truly transform reality,"[41] Paganism is radicalized as a societal catalyst. Snow confesses:

> From there, it's about power. It's about the power to create
> outcomes and wield change. . . . And, it's about the power it
> takes to make that happen. Because of that, witchcraft has
> always been something marginalized groups can and should
> wield. No one is more powerless than those living on the
> fringe of society, and that is where most queer people can be
> found . . . in these darkened shadows we learn to share, to
> love, and to thrive even in the worst of times. Those shadows

that we thrive in can remain powerful allies in our spell craft and are a form of shadow work.[42]

Finding solidarity in the fringes, Pagans, queers, and Critical Race Theorists can unite because they perceive a common oppressor—Christianity. Viewed as a 2,000-year-old white patriarchal power structure, the Christian faith is blamed for enslaving the masses and oppressing minorities, heathens, witches, and the sexually non-conforming. While these assertions may appear as liberal nonsense to some, if Christians are to earnestly engage in reaching post-Millennials, it's imperative that we genuinely consider these assertions and remain "ready at any time to give a defense"[43] of our faith.

CHRIST AS OPPRESSOR

"Apart from the Bible's heterogeneity and outright self-contradiction, allowing it to justify diverse and irreconcilable aims, the culprit is clearly the doctrine of faith itself,"[44] hurls philosopher and atheist Sam Harris as part of his indictment against Christianity. Harris, who has become a poster child for New Atheism, references everything from the Crusades to the Salem witch trials as evidence Christianity is a negative force in society. While more common today, it's important to recognize how novel accusations such as these are against the Christian faith—at least in the modern era.

For most of the last 2,000 years, Christianity has been celebrated as good news, liberating the captives and being a light in the darkness. Encompassing Christ's words in Luke 4, the body of Christ has served the world by declaring "good news to the poor," "release to the captives," "sight to the blind," freedom to the "oppressed," and "favor" upon all of God's people. More than words, the global church played a monumental role in the development of hospitals, schools, and orphanages. Even well-known agnostic and critical scholar of the Bible Bart Ehrman credits Christianity's role in the development of hospitals, admitting they "were a Christian invention," and praises believers' contributions in this arena as "the most important development in the Christian history of charity."[45]

Deserving additional praise is Christianity's contributions to innovation. Influencing both the Enlightenment and the Industrial Revolution, Christian thinkers like Johannes Gutenberg, Alexander Graham Bell, Louis Pasteur, Samuel Morse, George Washington Carver, and Thomas Edison collectively shaped the modern world.* Their pioneering efforts encompass significant scientific advancements, including the discovery of the laws of motion and electricity, as well as the invention of the motion picture camera, advancements in agriculture such as crop rotation techniques, the development of Morse code and the telegraph, vaccination, pasteurization, and the invention of the telephone. Christianity served as a unifying foundation that inspired these individuals to apply their talents and insights toward advancing human knowledge and improving society.

Such is the hatred for Christ by modern Pagans that these beneficial contributions are vastly ignored and eclipsed by unfounded accusations of patriarchal dominance, justifying global conflicts, and condoning hate crimes against the LGBTQ+ community. Simultaneously forgotten are the historical sins of Pagan peoples, including the Diocletian Persecution, Viking raids on Christian monasteries, and the atrocities committed during the Holocaust, where over six million Jews were slaughtered under the occultic

---

* Alexander Graham Bell and Thomas Edison were both raised in a Christian household, but later distanced themselves from organized religion.

ideology of the Third Reich. And let's not forget to mention the continued Pagan-inspired abortion industry, which is responsible for the deaths of over 62 million children since *Roe v. Wade* became law in 1973.[46]

Recapitulating the societal grievances against the Christian faith, Chaz Bufe, author of *The Heretics Guide to the Bible* and *Listen, Anarchist*, asserts in his pamphlet *20 Reasons to Abandon Christianity* that Christianity "breeds authoritarianism," is "misogynistic," "homophobic," "extremely egocentric," and "based on dishonesty," and "encourages acceptance of real evils."[47] Reminiscent of the repudiations of Ancient Rome against Christianity, Harris and Bufe remind us that the Pagan world has always hated Christ and all who follow Him. From the church's inception, Christians faced accusations of cannibalism for consuming the "body and blood" of Christ, and atheism for refusing to worship the deities of Rome, and were even blamed for economic issues and losses on the battlefield.

As similar accusations against Christians resurface in the modern world, believers are reminded of Jesus' words in John 15:

> If the world hates you, understand that it hated me before it hated you. If you were of the world, the world would love you as its own. However, because you are not of the world, but I have chosen you out of it, the world hates you. Remember the word I spoke to you: "A servant is not greater than his master." If they persecuted me, they will also persecute you. If they kept my word, they will also keep yours. But they will do all these things to you on account of my name . . .[48]

Identifying the crux of the issue, Jesus rightly highlights that Christians are hated, only because He is hated first. To a people who are perishing, akin to the demons who cried out, "Have you

22

come here to torment us before the time?"[49] Christ is viewed as a tyrant, at the ready with punishment and judgment. Failing to grasp His boundless compassion, those who oppose Him lash out, hurl insults, persecute prophets, build towers, seek power, and wage war against His name.

For our TikTok influencer, Thorn, this may look like ritualistic defiance against the Christian faith. For a media juggernaut like Disney, this will result in creating content designed to desensitize the younger generation to anti-God ideologies. For Marxist activists like Snow and Guerra-Lorenzo, they will stop at nothing to train radical extremists against a perceived Christian hegemony. But no matter what the Pagan threat against Christians looks like, one thing is certain: If Christ is the oppressor, eventually Satan will be viewed as the Liberator.

TWO

LILITH
AND LUCIFER

MISUNDERSTOOD DREAMERS

"We'll show Heaven a fight they won't forget!"[1] defiantly declares an animated character in Vivienne Medrano's (also known as "VivziePop") new #1 adult-targeted dark-comedy Amazon series *Hazbin Hotel*.

The raunchy series follows Charlie, the princess of Hell, as she seeks to rehabilitate demons to prevent overpopulation in her fiery abode. The show, which features, as one character describes, "blood, violence, and depravity of a sexual nature,"[2] is laced with expletives, musical numbers, and inappropriate material lived out by a disturbing bunch of animated inhabitants of Hell, including Charlie's lesbian partner "Vaggie," and a porn-star named "Angel Dust."[3] The show, which claims to be an "adult animated musical series,"[4] is available free of charge to all Amazon Prime members, making it easily accessible to children and younger audiences.

Even more disturbing is how the show positions Lucifer and other demons, including Adam's supposed first wife-turned-demon and lover of Lucifer, Lilith, as misunderstood dreamers, with genuinely good intentions "to share the magic of free will with humanity."[5] The introduction of the first episode depicts Lucifer's fall from Heaven:

Once upon a time, there was a glowing city protected by
golden gates, known as "heaven." It was ruled by beings of
pure light, angels that worshiped good and shielded all from
evil. Lucifer was one of these angels. He was a dreamer, with
fantastical ideas for all of creation, but he was seen as a
troublemaker by the elders of Heaven. For they felt his way
of thinking was dangerous to the order of their world . . . as
punishment for their reckless act, heaven cast Lucifer and
his love in the dark pit that he had created. Never allowing
him to see the good that came from humanity, only the cruel
and the wicked. Ashamed, Lucifer lost his will to dream, but
Lilith thrived. . . .

Contrasting the biblical account, in Medrano's new show, heaven is ruled by elders and angels, without mentioning the Father, Son, or Holy Spirit. These "beings of pure light" created the world, but ruled over it with a heavy hand, depriving humanity of free will. Lucifer, described in the show's opener, as the creative, compassionate, and caring rebel, revolted against the elder's wishes and gifted free will to Adam and his wife, Lilith. Close-minded and judgmental, these elders punish the misunderstood and benevolent Lucifer for this subversive act. For Medrano, her Lucifer isn't evil; he's a Marx-like revolutionary, who stood up to power and resisted the patriarchal elders to liberate Lilith, the woman he loves.

This animated series is just another example of Hollywood's attempt to groom young audiences with a toxic concoction of feminist dogma, queer theory, and Marxist propaganda. At its core is a godless Pagan tale, which glorifies Hell, demons, and the devil himself. While praised for its originality, *Hazbin Hotel's* distorted premise, as we will soon see, is anything but new.

THE NIGHT SPIRIT

Long before VivziePop's modern animated interpretation, a mythology of Lilith as Adam's first wife circulated in Jewish folklore and later in proto-feminist writings. Completely absent of biblical corroboration, the earliest known reference exists in a satirical pseudepigraphical medieval work known as the Alphabet of Ben Sira. Dated to sometime between the eighth and tenth century AD, the Alphabet of Ben Sira provides a subversive reading of the creation accounts of mankind in Genesis, specifically Genesis 1:27 and Genesis 2:21-22. Rather than viewing these passages through the lens of orthodoxy as two separate descriptions of a unified narrative, the Alphabet of Ben Sira (and the later feminist theory it inspired) separates the accounts into two unique and subsequent events believed to describe the creation of Lilith from the dust alongside Adam, and then later, Eve, from his rib.

According to the Alphabet of Ben Sira, Adam's first wife, Lilith, was created at the same time and from the same earth as Adam and was made to be his equal. However, a conflict arose between Adam and Lilith over the issue of equality and submission:

> *[Adam and Lilith] promptly began to argue with each other: She said, "I will not lie below," and he said, "I will not lie below, but above since you are fit for being below and I for being above." She said to him, "The two of us are equal since we are both from the earth." And they would not listen to each other. Since Lilith saw [how it was], she uttered God's ineffable name and flew away into the air.*[6]

Lilith's refusal to submit to Adam during intercourse marked her rebellion against his dominance, establishing her as the first to defy patriarchal authority. Later in the medieval account and consistent with *Hazbin Hotel's* narrative, Lilith lies with the "Great Demon"[7] Lucifer and is eventually transformed into a demon spirit herself. This association of Lilith, the wife of Adam, as a demon spirit, is likely the combination of ancient mythologies, Jewish folklore, and a single verse from the Bible.

While scripture makes no mention of Adam having any other wives, nor of a specific woman named Lilith, there is a single mention of a creature of the night in Isaiah 34:14 called "Lilith" (תִּילִיל):

> *The creatures of the desert will encounter jackals*
> *And the hairy goat will call to its kind;*
> *Indeed, Lilith (night demon) will settle there*
> *And find herself a place of rest.*[8]

While other translations of the same passage are less mysterious and utilize the word "owl" or "screech owl" in place of "lilith," the association in the Hebrew language of a night spirit finds support in other ancient texts of "lilith" spirits, known as, "lilitu" or "lili-demons," that roam the night, preying on men and infants. According to Old Testament scholar Dr. Michael Heiser, "Biblical writers were not expressing the notion that night birds ... were actually demons,"[9] but rather, he explains, the Bible uses prophetic language to describe actual demonic entities that dwell in spiritually desolate realms. Offering broader support for these creatures, J.A. Scurlock presents evidence of "lilith's" presence in ancient Mesopotamian texts as well:

> *The lilû-demons and their female counterparts the lilitu or*
> *ardat lili-demons were hungry for victims because they had*
> *once been human; they were the spirits of young men and*
> *women who had themselves died young. If a girl had the*
> *misfortune of dying before she had the opportunity to marry*

or have children, it was believed that her ghost was forever
doomed to prowl the earth in the form of a lilitu or ardat
lili-demon.[10]

The evolution of this hybridization of Lilith as a rebellious and independent figure who defies patriarchal authority, and transforms into a powerful demonic spirit being, has made her a symbol in various occultic feminist writings and interpretations. This is further emphasized by the figure of Lucifer, whose own story of defiance and fall from grace parallels that of Lilith. In many variations of the myth, Lucifer is seen as empowering Lilith, offering her support and an alternative to the subjugation she faced. This connection between Lilith and Lucifer further cements her status as a symbol of rebellion and resistance. Through Lucifer, Lilith finds an ally who embodies the struggle against oppressive structures, thus entangling their fates and amplifying their significance in feminist reinterpretations. Per Faxneld, a historian of religions and expert on Western esotericism, explores further "how the devil can be conceptualized as women's helper" in *Satanic Feminism*, stating:

> *Some women (and the occasional man), typically influenced*
> *by the Romantic's transformation of Satan into a hero,*
> *now performed counter readings of Christian misogynist*
> *traditions. Hereby, Lucifer became reconceptualized as a*
> *feminist liberator of womankind. In these counter-myths,*
> *he is seen as an ally in the struggle against a patriarchy*
> *supported by God the Father and his male priests. Eve's*
> *ingestion of the forbidden fruit becomes a heroic act of*
> *rebellion against the tyranny of God and Adam.*[11]

Building on these reinterpretations of mythological and biblical figures, first-wave feminists, such as Mary Wollstonecraft,

Susan B. Anthony, and Elizabeth Cady Stanton, utilized a revisionist approach to dismantling orthodox interpretations of women's
roles in biblical texts, advocating instead for readings that affirmed
women's agency and equality, and, oftentimes, their supremacy
over men. To do so, women must become "liberated," not only of
a perceived patriarchy but of their very humanity. This shift from
human to divine is the epitome of the Marxist and Pagan intersection within feminist thought. Within this view, for a woman to
be liberated, she must be elevated above mankind into the form
of a goddess. Therefore, as explained by Rachel Wilson, author of
Occult Feminism: The Secret History of Women's Liberation, feminism is inseparable from Paganism:

> *This is the reason feminism is born of occult belief, because
> at its core, feminism seeks to make women gods over men, or
> at the very least to deify women. The very essence of feminist
> thought is a worldview where women and men struggle for
> dominance. This is the Hegelian master-slave dialectic, and
> it defines the feminist struggle no matter how often feminists
> want to convince us that it's about equality.*[12]

For Hegel, a struggle for dominance, and not equality, is the
expected outcome of two self-conscious beings encountering one
another, as was displayed in the story of Adam and Lilith. Within
Pagan feminism, there can be no compromise or appreciation of
one another for the uniqueness of each sex, only a fight for power.
This fight for power may have been fueled by the figures of Lilith
and Lucifer, who represent defiance and rebellion against patriarchal structures. However, for feminists to expect to take any
ground, they must first deconstruct Christian tradition and the
Bible itself. It was Elizabeth Cady Stanton and her work on *The
Woman's Bible* that took on this task, echoing the defiance seen in

the reinterpretations of Lilith and Lucifer, while simultaneously adopting a revisionist position toward the Bible itself, which, sadly, proved to be very effective.

THE WOMEN'S BIBLE

"Exonerate the snake, emancipate the women,"[13] writes Elizabeth Cady Stanton, a dominant figure in first-wave feminism and the suffrage movement, in her 1895 book, *The Woman's Bible.* Stanton, who was a contemporary suffragist of Susan B. Anthony and impacted by Pagan ideas, gathered 24 other feminist activists to produce a counterreading of the Bible "to revise . . . texts and chapters directly referring to women."[14] Driving her subversive translations of the text was what Wilson calls her "fundamental opposition to Christianity"[15] wherein Stanton saw Christian orthodoxy as "the only thing holding back women's liberation."[16]

Stanton's all-female revising committee, made up of Christian scientists, mediums, spiritualists, occultists, and atheists, were all radical feminists and profoundly progressive.[17] Their main priority was to deconstruct traditional understandings of Biblical passages that they perceived contributed to the oppression of women or the furtherance of the patriarchy. Topping their list were the topics of creation, marriage, submission, sexuality, childbirth, and even the Trinity, which the committee criticized for not possessing a female person.

To solve this, Stanton introduced the heretical idea of a "feminine element"[18] into the Trinity in the form of a "Heavenly Father, Mother, and Son," which she reasoned, " . . . would seem more rational."[19] Further speculating, "The first step in the elevation of woman to her true position, as an equal factor in human progress, is the cultivation of the religious sentiment in regard to her dignity and equality, the recognition by the rising generation of an ideal Heavenly Mother."[20] Stanton reasoned that since God had created man in His own image, making male and female, the Godhead must contain a feminine element "equal in power and glory with the masculine."[21]

For Stanton, it was "the church and clergy" who made women's "emancipation impossible."[22] Despite ample evidence of strong female figures located within the scriptures (like Miriam, Deborah, Esther, Priscilla, and Phoebe, to name a few) Stanton felt that the Bible painted the fairer sex as a "mournful object of pity" so much so that she jests it would take "the occult mystic power of the eastern Mahatmas"[23] to "transpose and transfigure" her into a specimen "worthy our worship."[24] This may have been tongue-in-cheek for Stanton, but a later feminist leader, Helena Petrovna Blavatsky (commonly known as Madame Blavatsky) seemed to take the invitation to merge feminist ideas with occult beliefs to challenge the patriarchy and liberate women's goddess status as a literal challenge.

MADAME BLAVATSKY

Spinning tales of global travel and supernatural encounters, Helena Petrovna Blavatsky (1831–1891), the matriarch of Theosophy, "came from a long line of wealthy aristocrats and nobles from Russia and Europe."[25] Relying upon her "interior man,"[26] or spirit guide, Blavatsky claimed supernatural powers, such as "clairvoyance, astral projection, telepathy, and the ability to psychically teleport objects."[27] Perhaps best remembered as the founder of the Theosophical Society, Madame Blavatsky was notably influenced by the socialist-inspired esoteric teachings of Alphonse Louis Constant, otherwise known as Éliphas Lévi, who himself had been deeply impacted by the utopian socialist ideas of Henri de Saint-Simon, which I wrote about in-depth in my book, *The Christian Left*.[28] Though Blavatsky "despised the Christian idea of a personal God"[29] and considered the Christian faith "fiction,"[30] she praised Jesus as "the great Socialist and Adept"[31] and further perpetuated the heretical idea that Satan was a Promethean-like hero, who delivered not fire, but free-will to man in the form of the knowledge of good and evil.

> *In this case, it is but natural—even from the dead-letter standpoint—to view Satan, the Serpent of Genesis, as the real creator and benefactor, the Father of Spiritual Mankind. For it is he who was the "Harbinger of Light," bright radiant Lucifer, who opened the eyes of the automaton "created" by Jehovah, as alleged. And he who was the first to whisper, "in the day ye eat thereof ye shall be as Elohim, knowing good and evil," can only be regarded in the light of a Saviour.*[32]

Blavatsky, who dismissed Charles Darwin's theory of evolution, reasoned that just as Prometheus stole "the Divine Fire so as to allow men to proceed consciously on the path of Spiritual Evolution, thus transforming the most perfect of animals on Earth into a potential God . . . "[33] and was cursed by Zeus; Lucifer, likewise, heroically accepted the punishment of the curse for granting enlightenment to humanity. For Blavatsky, who promoted the idea of reincarnation, this "spiritual evolution" granted by Lucifer made gradual enlightenment over multiple lifetimes to a higher state of consciousness until one reached a place of spiritual mastery, transforming them into a "guru," "master," or "adept,"[34] possible. Accumulating a significant following, particularly among the elite, Blavatsky's theosophical ideas paved the way for a more widespread form of universalism, where global religions could be synthesized by interpreting figures like Jesus, Buddha, and Mohammad as all achieving master status.

Like Stanton's "feminine element," Blavatsky's spiritual framework incorporated the importance of the divine feminine. She frequently referenced goddesses from various mythologies, such as Isis from Egyptian mythology,[35] Ishtar from Mesopotamian mythology,[36] and Kali from Hindu mythology.[37] These goddesses, embodying wisdom, power, and transformation, represented the divine feminine principle that Blavatsky believed was crucial for spiritual revolution. In her view, embracing the divine feminine was essential for progressing humanity toward what she called "dual transformation,"[38] a form of spiritual and physical evolution, restoring us back to our original primordial state and divine nature. Guiding and nurturing this process was what Blavatsky called the Universal Mother, who "being before the sun, she almost eclipses its light." Pontificating on what she believed was the interconnected and universal role of the divine feminine, she added, " . . . nothing could more completely identify the Christian mother and child with Isis and Horus, Ishtar, Venus, Juno, and a host of other Pagan goddesses, who have been called 'Queen of Heaven,' 'Queen of the Universe,' 'Mother of God,' 'Spouse of God,' 'the Celestial Virgin,' 'the Heavenly Peace-Maker,' etc."[39] This misguided reverence for the goddess archetype underscored her blasphemous belief that spiritual progress involved not only the recognition of masculine divinity but also the empowerment and deification of the feminine.

While Blavatsky's theosophical tenets are nearly 150 years old, their influence remains strong, acting as a silent satanic sherpa guiding today's feminist and Woke warriors toward her distorted evolutionary enlightenment. Her concepts of spiritual evolution and goddess worship, combined with her disdain for biblical Christianity, undergird America's religious zeitgeist and have almost single-handedly shaped feminine pop culture.

GODDESS WORSHIP

In 2018, San Francisco's Grace Cathedral hosted "Beyoncé Mass," advertised as "a womanist worship service."[40] The religious experience, which was organized by Reverend and theologian Yolanda Norton and featured the music of pop icon Beyoncé Giselle Knowles-Carter, was described by Wesleyan University board member, Nyasha Shani Foi, who supported the event, as primarily for "women of color, but for anyone who happens to sing praises to the goddess herself, Beyoncé."[41] Not even hiding their goddess worship and affinity for Marxist ideology, the organizers behind "Beyoncé Mass" described the event on their website as "how black women find their voice, represent the image of God, and create spaces for liberation."[42]

"Beyoncé Mass" wasn't the first group to elevate the globally recognized artist to goddess status. In 2013, a group of her followers in Atlanta founded The National Church of Bey,[43] boasting the birth of a new religion, known as Beyism, dedicated to "worshiping the sanctity of the Mother Bey." While it's unclear whether The National Church of Bey, which has no formal affiliation to the artist herself, is a religious joke or not,[44] there is no shortage of idolizing comments directed to her on the popular social media platform X.

Spiritual praises she's received include:

- "Whatever this new religion is, @Beyonce, we shall worship at its altar. #Grammys #Beyonce #goddess"
  —The official Playboy X page @playboy[45]
- "Beyoncé is like the literal definition of mother goddess supreme and she will ALWAYS be mother goddess supreme."
  —@crdanexo[46]

- "Okay everybody repeat after me: God is a woman and her name is Beyoncé Giselle Knowles Carter."
  —@beyoncesdealer[47]

While Beyoncé may not have endorsed cult worship directly, the themes of her music, lyrics, and concert imagery certainly seem to invite the practice. Reviewing the visuals of her 2016 album *Lemonade*, which features lyrics like, "When you love me, you love yourself/Love God herself," professor and *Time* magazine contributor, Omise'eke Natasha Tinsley identifies that Beyoncé processes through "infidelity, hurt, and transcendence"[48] as she appears as "a parade of black Atlantic deities," such as the Nigerian fertility goddess Oshun, the Egyptian queen-deity Nefertiti, and Erzulie Red-Eyes, a Haitian feminine Vodou spirit known as "the only woman" with the power to enslave, rape, and kill men. Offering a definitive observance of Beyoncé's spiritual evolution, Tinsley writes in a manner that almost feels like a confession of faith:

> Beyoncé's Lemonade *is grown-ass black woman magic. And the lemons that Queen Bey is working with, powerful hoodoo ingredients for overpowering bad energy, are clearly the Louisiana kind. Lush, troubling visuals show that Beyoncé is the goddess, the goddess is furious, the goddess is victorious, and most important: The goddess is every black woman. Slay.*

What's more, goddess worship doesn't start or stop with Beyoncé. Rivaling her divine status is Country music artist turned pop sensation Taylor Swift. In May 2024, around 1,200 "Swifties" gathered in a 600-year-old Heidelberg church, The Church of the Holy Spirit, for a rainbow flying T-Swift-themed worship experience titled "Anti-Hero—Taylor Swift Church Service." Pastor

Vincenzo Petracca used the service to highlight Swift's lyrics and their ties to "social justice causes like feminism and racism as ways she exhibits her faith."[49]

The pop singer, who boasts of her "Tennessee Christian values,"[50] revealed her scorn against the Christian faith in her recent album, *The Tortured Poets Department,* in which she seems to portray Christians as "hateful and judgmental,"[51] with lyrics like, "You ain't gotta pray for me" and "What if I roll the stone away?/ They're gonna crucify me anyway/What if the way you hold me is actually what's holy."[52] Whether the blonde-haired tortured poet will fully abandon her Christian roots is yet to be seen, but for now, she seems to be satisfied leveraging her form of Christianity when it's convenient, while simultaneously implying true believers are close-minded and judgmental for not accepting her progressive ideologies. This is exactly what she did in Tennessee when she went against Sen. Marsha Blackburn for her support of traditional marriage and pro-life values. Swift responded,

It's right and wrong at this point, and I can't see another commercial and see her disguising these policies behind the words "Tennessee Christian values." Those aren't Tennessee Christian values . . . I live in Tennessee. I am Christian. That's not what we stand for.[53]

Swift was recently accused of making an even bolder statement when she invited rapper and friend Ice Spice (whose real name is Isis Naija Gaston) to accompany her to the 2024 Super Bowl. During the game, Gaston, dressed in Balenciaga, flashed what some believed were "devil's horns" while wearing an alleged satanic cross necklace.[54] Similar accusations have been made in the past toward Nicki Minaj, Lady Gaga, and Beyoncé.[55] More frightening is the fact that each of these female artists, much like

Blavatsky's "interior man," claims to have an alter ego or spirit guide that either takes over or assists them somehow in their creative process. Minaj goes as far as to call hers a demon named Roman. Eerily explaining his existence, she offered:

> *Roman is a crazy boy who lives in me. And he says the things*
> *that I don't want to say. He was born . . . just a few months*
> *ago. He was conceived in rage, so he bashes everyone. He*
> *wants to be blamed. I don't blame him. I asked him to leave,*
> *but he can't. He's here for a reason. People have brought him*
> *out, now he won't leave.*[56]

Much like the story of Lilith, it seems that the deification that Lucifer offers has its disadvantages. Though these women may have found fame and fortune, the looming question is, "At what expense?" Each of these women is idolized, deified by the world, and revered as a modern goddess. However, this adoration often comes at the cost of their emotional and spiritual well-being, as they are dragged deeper into a perverse and twisted industry that seeks to transform artists into Pagan activists who parade their bodies on stages while their followers raise their hands in blind worship.

This pattern of deification extends beyond music and entertainment. As these women parade their bodies on stage, their performances blur the line between vulgar entertainment and something far worse—a ritualistic celebration of self-worship and spiritual rebellion. What began as the feminist pursuit of autonomy has, in many cases, led to a grotesque inversion of its original goals. Instead of achieving true liberation, these artists indulge and deepen the fantasies of the very men they claim to reject. The irony is glaring: in their quest to "own" their bodies and break free from male dominance, they become spectacles of objectification, exalted not for their minds or achievements, but for their ability to seduce and transgress.

Nowhere was this more evident than at the 2025 Grammys, where Kanye West's wife, Australian model Bianca Censori, made a shocking fashion statement. Arriving in a black oversized fur coat, she quickly shed it as she stepped onto the red carpet to reveal "a completely see-through dress seemingly crafted from sheer stockings . . . leaving nothing to the imagination."[57] The moment was a twisted display of modern feminism's descent into self-parody—what was once a movement for dignity and respect has become a desperate exhibition for attention framed as empowerment.

And when these men—stripped of the courage to step into their God-given role for fear of offending a feminist—turn elsewhere for satisfaction, they find a world equally twisted: the porn industry. Here, the so-called empowerment of women takes a darker turn, offering yet another perverse mirage of freedom.

WOMEN IN PORN: LIBERATION OR ULTIMATE OPPRESSION?

"Sex has historically been a commodity. It's a valuable source of power. . . . Sexual power is . . . the female commodity," states Carol Cassell (qtd. in Strossen 123) in her book *Swept Away: Why Women Confuse Love and Sex*.[58] Challenging the traditional feminist position that pornography subjugates women as it often involves the commodification of female bodies as an object of male pleasure, Nadine Strossen in her book, *Defending Pornography: Free Speech, Sex, and the Fight for Women's Rights*, makes the case that pornography serves "to educate, liberate, and empower."[59] Marking a decisive shift in the historical dialectic of feminist thought, Harvard-educated Strossen is one of many sex-positive feminists to suggest that pornography empowers women by providing a platform for sexual expression, challenging traditional norms, and asserting autonomy over their bodies and desires. Simply put, for sex-positive feminists like Strossen, pornography is a means to overthrow the patriarchy and elevate women as goddesses who rule over men.

One such platform amplifying so-called female sexual empowerment in the digital age is OnlyFans, a subscription-based website that allows "content creators" to build an audience and directly charge viewers for access to unrestricted content. Whereas in ancient times, particularly in Pagan Rome, sex workers were often viewed as "effectively subhumans"[60] and existed on the fringes of society, today top OnlyFans models like Mia Khalifa, reportedly earn over $5 million a month,[61] placing them among the highest earners in the country. Attempting to normalize the practice, the porn industry has introduced terminology like, *adult entertainer*, *performer*, or *model*, to replace more crude-sounding monikers, such as *sex worker* and *prostitute*. The growing cultural acceptance of sexual deviance has allowed many women and men to proudly display their *performance* links and subscription information on their social media sites for all to see, something that previously would have been reserved for the back rooms and alleyways of American culture.

The combination of high earning potential, complete autonomy, and increasing social acceptance has led to more than two million[62] creators joining the website, many of them being young women aged 20–40, with the average age reported to be 29.[63] "In the same way that many young men fall into porn addiction by first looking at bikini photos, then graduating to fully nude images. . . . Many women start out on OnlyFans as an experiment with innocent intentions,"[64] writes Andrew Ferebee in an online article entitled *Clicks, Cash, and Consequences: How OnlyFans Affects Women's Lives, Relationships, Social Value, and Future Opportunities*. Addressing the epidemic at which young women are being drawn into the platform, he writes:

> In the beginning, it's just a fun and playful way to make an extra income doing something she enjoys like "modeling" and her content mirrors the content on her social media channels with slightly better angles. She isn't revealing much. Just a few bikini photos that she already has on her phone. As soon as a creator has hooked their audience and begun to earn money and followers, it becomes increasingly difficult to stay relevant and maintain earnings with the same bikini photos or level of sensual content that may have worked in the beginning. It's human nature to always want more. And we see this nature on display from both the creators and consumers of OnlyFans.[65]

A far cry from the promises of spiritual evolution touted by Blavatsky, Ferebee reveals the dark and dangerous devolution that likely awaits those who dip their toes into satanic feminism. Like the legend of Lilith, there is a fall that awaits all those who rebel against God's precepts and align their hearts with Lucifer's lies. With promises of money, power, and pleasure, it's easy to see how pornography has become Satan's perfect weapon ensnaring millions of people of all ages and both sexes into a life of addiction, sexual perversion, and idol worship. While it may trigger a temporary dopamine hit, pornography is a fantasy, and a false one at that. As Proverbs reminds us regarding "the lips of the forbidden woman . . . in the end she's as bitter as wormwood, . . . Her feet go down to death; her steps head straight for Sheol."[66]

EMPOWERMENT ENDS IN ENSLAVEMENT

From a conservative Christian perspective, the rise of goddess worship and the mainstream embrace of pornography are not mere cultural shifts—they are symptoms of an ancient rebellion repackaged for modern consumption. The Old Testament is filled with warnings about idolatry, not because God is insecure, but because He understands the human tendency to trade the truth for a lie and to exchange the glory of the Creator for the seduction of the created.

Time and again, Israel fell into the worship of Asherah, Ishtar, and other fertility goddesses, not simply because of theological confusion, but because these cults promised pleasure without consequence and power without righteousness. The same dynamic is at work today. The adoration of celebrities as divine figures, the ritualistic performances on stage, and the unabashed commodification of the human body all echo the same Pagan errors of the past.

But history is nothing if not repetitive. What begins as empowerment often ends in enslavement. The worship of self, whether through the deification of pop stars or the so-called liberation of pornography, does not elevate—it degrades. It promises freedom but delivers bondage, not only for those who participate but for the entire culture that bows to its altar. As ancient Israel learned the hard way, a people who abandon God do not remain free for long. Consider these two examples:

- *Asherah and Baal Worship.* The Old Testament frequently condemns the worship of Asherah, a Canaanite goddess associated with fertility, and Baal, a storm and fertility god. The Israelites' adoption of these deities' worship practices led to their downfall and divine judgment, as seen in the Books of Judges and Kings. The prophet Jeremiah specifically condemns the worship of the "Queen of Heaven," a title often associated with Asherah (Jeremiah 7:18, 44:17-19).

- *Solomon's Apostasy.* King Solomon, despite his wisdom, fell into idolatry by accommodating his foreign wives' worship of other gods, including Ashtoreth (1 Kings 11:1-13). This led to the division of his kingdom and is a warning against syncretism and the dangers of departing from exclusive worship of Yahweh.

These examples reveal a clear pattern: When a nation turns to idols, it does not remain spiritually or morally intact. This cycle of false empowerment, built on the worship of idols and the degradation of the human body, naturally paves the way for an even more demonic manifestation of power—a power that seeks control over life itself.

This shift from sexual freedom to sexual dominance leads inexorably to the ultimate act of control: Abortion. Just as ancient deities demanded sacrifices, the modern goddess movement claims its power through the blood of the innocent.

GODDESS POWER: REPRODUCTIVE RIGHTS FOR ALL

Tracing the spiritual evolution of satanic feminists, the path moves from liberation to traditional gender roles to sexual freedom, then to sexual dominance, and ultimately to exercising control over life itself through abortion. This last step, the intentional slaughter of an unborn child, serves as a "necessary" ceremonial act to solidify one's godlikeness. After all, without a sacrifice, there can be no deity.

"My fetus dancing right before it was aborted" appears as text on a screen in a 2024 TikTok video,[67] while a young woman dances on camera in a crop top shirt. This content creator, known by the social media handle @abortioncounselor, is one of thousands using social media to flaunt and glorify the slaughter of their innocent unborn children. Lacking all regard for human life, these creators affirm Pagan scholar and author Ginette Paris' confession from her book, *The Sacrament of Abortion*, that abortion, at its deepest level, is a Pagan act "necessary to sacrifice the fetus to a higher cause."[68]

As a modern feminist, Paris seems willing to say what those before her were more reticent to admit—that abortion is really a Pagan sacrifice; a religious act. "Abortion as a sacrifice to Artemis. Abortion as a sacrament," she explains, "for the gift of life to remain pure."[69] Relying upon a Pagan dialectic to justify the horrific practice of abortion, Paris desires "to restore abortion to its sacred dimension."[70]

Keep in mind, though, that sacred doesn't mean moral. In fact, Margaret Sanger, famed eugenicist and founder of Planned Parenthood, criticized Marxism "not because of its . . . revolutionary character,"[71] but because of its dependence upon "moral fervor and enthusiasm."[72] For Sanger, Marx was not heartless enough. She believed he lacked the somber, moralless fortitude required to truly effect revolutionary change, which she saw as "sexual"[73] in origin. In her view, it was the proletariat, not the bourgeoisie, who were complicit in their own oppression by continually supplying the bourgeoisie with a readily available "labor surplus."[74] Thus for Sanger, a member of the Socialist Party,[75] the only way forward for Marxist revolution was to embrace her brand of radical feminism, seizing the highest form of the means of production—life itself.

In the prologue to Sanger's book *Woman and the New Race,* British sexologist and social reformer Havelock Ellis exposes how feminism, what he calls "the woman movement," and Marxist ideology via the "Labour movement," are necessary allies in the evolutionary path of societal reform. For Ellis, who was "among the first to suggest that homosexuality is not a disease, but a 'natural' harmless quirk,"[76] women held the key to directing the future state of society, as they ultimately control human production:

> *One final step remained to be taken—it had to be realised not only that the Labour movement could give the secret of success to the woman movement by its method and organization, but that on the other hand, women held the secret without which labour is impotent to reach its ends. Woman, by virtue of motherhood, is the regulator of the birthrate, the sacred disposer of human production. It is in the deliberate restraint and measurement of human production that the fundamental problems of the family, the nation, the whole brotherhood of mankind find their solution. The health and longevity of the individual, the economic welfare of the workers, the general level of culture of the community, the possibility of abolishing from the world the desolating scourge of war—all these like great human needs, depend, primarily and fundamentally, on the wise limitation of the human output.*

According to Ellis, as regulators of the birth rate, what he calls "human output," women control the workers, the economy, and even global conflict—essentially everything! By embodying this "sacred" role, the feminine element achieves the next step in her transformation into a deity, elevating "liberated" women to goddess status. In a sick, twisted spiritual comparison, theosophical

Marxist copycats seem to reason that because God gave "His one and only Son"[78] and thus demonstrated His deity, their own "choice" to abort their baby proves their own god-likeness.

Unfortunately, though, the Pagan lust for power and divinity doesn't stop there. Like Simon the Sorcerer in the Book of Acts, today's neo-Pagans and Satanists want more control and more power, and as we will see, for many, this means experimenting with hallucinogenic drugs and the worship of otherworldly powers to connect with the ultimate goddess—Mother Earth.

THREE

COSMIC UTOPIA: EARTH GODDESSES AND ALIEN WORSHIP

HUMANS ARE A VIRUS

"**S**ome environmentalists now speak of Gaia as a real presence, similar to a universal spirit or the 'world soul' of Plato's metaphysics. In Green-speak, she maintains Earth's equilibrium—even at the expense of us, the only inhabitants on the planet conscious of her existence,"[1] wrote Joe Humphrey, assistant news editor at *The Irish Times* in an article titled "God, Make Way for Gaia: A Deity Even Atheists Can Believe In."

Humphrey quoted Regius Professor of Greek at Trinity College Dublin John Dillon, who explained that Gaia, a "lustful, irritable and contrary"[2] goddess of Greek mythology, who is similar to Mother Earth:

> *is not a malevolent force, but she is concerned to protect*
> *the climatic equilibrium that she has established over many*
> *millennia, and if she identifies us, the human species, as*
> *a virus that is likely to disrupt, and even destroy, that*
> *equilibrium, through our reckless greed and devotion to*
> *infinite, exponential "growth," she will take steps, either to*
> *eliminate us altogether or to cut us very much down to size.*[3]

Thus, worshipers of Gaia, who can be found in both climate science and various shamanistic practices, are influenced by the myth of overpopulation and tend to see the Earth "as a living system" and humanity as a threat to the balance of equilibrium. Contrasting God's commission in Genesis 1 to, "be fruitful, multiply, fill the earth, and subdue it," adherents to Gaia see humanity as a parasite, advocating for stringent population control and radical environmental measures, which further explains the religious-like devotion radicals on the left maintain toward abortion and green policies. Regarding these Earth worshipers, author of *Occult Feminism* Rachel Wilson brings to light that "all share the same worldview and perception of humanity as a scourge on the planet which must be managed, controlled, and reduced by the ruling class who have combined ancient occult beliefs . . . to produce anti-Christian, anti-human ideas about what the world should be."[4]

The British economist Thomas Malthus, in his 1798 work *An Essay on the Principle of Population*, first planted the seeds of this flawed perspective in the anxious minds of today's Leftists when he wrote "that the power of population is indefinitely greater than the power in the earth to produce subsistence for man." He believed that overpopulation was the root cause of disease, hunger, and war and that preventing population growth was the primary solution. His unfounded and pessimistic ideas, referred to today as "Malthusian," continue to guide many of the policies and positions on the Left, including "green" initiatives, abortion practices, depopulation measures, and so-called "wealth redistribution" politics. Though a Christian himself, Malthus' ideas were often at odds with traditional Christian beliefs, and directly influenced future eugenicists, like Planned Parenthood's founder Margaret Sanger and, worse, the Nazi regime.[5] While corrupt world leaders have used Malthus' ideas to frighten and coerce the masses (i.e., China's one-child policy), modern research has proven these ideas patently false.

Austin Ruse, author of *Fake Science: Exposing the Left's Skewed Statistics, Fuzzy Facts, and Dodgy Data*, reveals:

> *The claim that the world will become dangerously overpopulated has never been true. It was false when first postulated in the 19th century. It was false when The Population Bomb was first published in the 1960s. It is false now. That this theory is still taught in grade schools all over the world even today does not make it any truer. It remains a false theory.*[6]

Ruse points out that, contrary to Malthus' claims, fertility rates are "plummeting rapidly all over the world."[7] If anything, as Elon Musk and others have pointed out, "population collapse due to low birth rates is a much bigger risk to civilization"[8] than overpopulation. This is exactly what co-authors Marian Tupy and Gale L. Pooley document in their groundbreaking book, *Superabundance: The Story of Population Growth, Innovation, and Human Flourishing on an Infinitely Bountiful Planet*, in which they found that "additional human beings tend to benefit, rather than impoverish, the rest of humanity."[9]

Based on their research, Malthus was wrong. The more people there are, the more innovation there is . . . assuming that individuals were . . . "free to think, speak, read, publish, and interact with others."[10]

Despite the evidence, Malthusian ideas continue to be promoted by neo-Pagans and dystopian scientists who, in their warnings of an inevitable crisis, seek to appease Gaia, the Earth goddess, either literally or metaphorically. Here are a few examples of shocking claims made by climate alarmists in recent years:

- "Millennials and Gen Z and all these folks that come after us are looking up, and we're like, 'The world is going to end in 12 years if we don't address climate change, and your biggest issue is how are we gonna pay for it?'"[11]
  —Rep. Alexandria Ocasio-Cortez, D-N.Y., January 2019
- "If we continue at the rate we are now, by the year 2030 we will set off an irreversible chain reaction which will trigger events beyond human control. Then, there is no going back."[12]
  —Greta Thunberg, December 2019
- "But my fellow humans must learn to live in partnership with the Earth, otherwise the rest of creation will, as part of Gaia, unconsciously move the Earth to a new state in which humans may no longer be welcome. The virus, COVID-19, may well have been one negative feedback. Gaia will try harder next time with something even nastier."[13]
  —James Lovelock, November 2021

Taking the spirit of Malthus' ideas even further, Lovelock, a British environmentalist who first formulated Gaia Theory, held that "all life and all the material parts of the Earth's surface make up a single system, a kind of mega-organism, and a living planet."[14] Lovelock, as evidenced by his quote above, believed Gaia is a living earth and possesses a sort of universal mind, which must be appeased and satisfied through the service of humanity, or risk awakening her vengeance. Rather than the anthropocentric message of the Bible (in which humanity plays the central role within God's creation acting as a steward of the Earth until Christ's return), Lovelock introduced a self-regulating biocentric sentient planet that is pleased to annihilate humanity if we become a threat to her existence.

While Lovelock and Malthus' ideas may have been scientific in nature, their combined metaphysical implications of a looming existential threat and a living sentient earth were the lies needed to stoke the flames. Anti-Christian environmentalists and Pagan revivalists, who are focused on the worship of Gaia and the interconnectedness of the earth, now have the narrative for their quest to redefine spirituality and humanity's relationship to the world.

SORCERY AND THE GLOBAL DECEPTION

As if peering into the events of the Book of Revelation in real time, the rise of Earth-worshiping Pagan practices such as Wicca and witchcraft (which employ magical spells and curses, as well as hallucinogenic drugs) appears to signal that the great deception described in the Bible's final chapter may already be unfolding.

"It has fallen, Babylon the Great has fallen! She has become a home for demons, a haunt for every unclean spirit . . . because all the nations were deceived by your sorcery," prophesied John the Apostle in the Book of Revelation. According to John's prognostication, leading to the historic city's downfall was a great deception stemming from sorcery. According to Blue Letter Bible, an online Bible lexicon, the term "sorcery" (translated from the Greek word *pharmakeia*[15]) implies the manipulation and seduction of entire nations using magical arts and witchcraft and often relates to idolatry and the administering of mind-altering drugs,[16] ultimately leading to widespread spiritual and moral decay.

Demonstrating the manipulative and potential power of *pharmakeia*, the COVID-19 pandemic showed just how easy it is for mass psychosis to control the behavior of not only a single nation but the world. Borders closed, flights canceled, and citizens submitted en masse to a sole crazed power-hungry scientist attempting to hide his alleged role in fabricating a mysterious virus in a Wuhan lab. After watching more than 80% of Americans stand in line to receive a highly experimental dose of the COVID "vaccine,"[17] it's not hard to imagine how a future deception, driven by drugs, magic, and witchcraft, could once again deceive the nations—especially in the absence of the Christian faith. In fact, as Daniel Zomparelli reveals, the COVID-19 lockdowns may have even set the stage for the main event:

> *I was finally feeling more comfortable and less anxious about being in a new, big city in a new, big country—then the pandemic hit. Without warning, I felt farther away from my family than ever before with the border between America and Canada shut down. As someone who already suffers from very bad anxiety, I was struggling. So I did the only thing I could think of: ordered more candles and oils online.*[18]

Zomparelli detailed how the increased anxiety of the pandemic spurred his and his husband's interest in spellwork, crystals, and Pagan candles in his article, "The Pandemic Turned Me Into a Witch."

Having grown up in a Catholic home, Zomparelli had "given up on spirituality after trying to 'pray the gay away,'"[19] but was drawn to witchcraft during the pandemic because it provided "a sense of control amid chaos."[20] An example of Romans 1:28, "And because they did not think it worthwhile to acknowledge God, God delivered them over to a corrupt mind so that they do what is not right,"[21] Zomparelli is just one of tens of thousands of Christians who have tragically departed from the faith to pursue Pagan practices, like witchcraft and Wicca, and have fallen deeper into deception and depravity.

As Zomparelli points out, a major draw into witchcraft and spellwork for him was gaining a sense of control, which he attributed to alleviating his very bad anxiety. This sense of empowerment is a significant attraction for neo-Pagans who are looking for ways to handle the chaos and uncertainty of the modern world. Through countless spells, oils, the lighting of candles, and other practices, Pagans claim the power to affect various aspects of life through shamanistic powers, giving rise to even deeper deception. Consider the enticing language used in this advertisement for a Pagan practice, which promises mystery and magic, while subtly masking its dark source of power:

> Join us as we explore shamanic practices that bring you
> into the underworld and the deepest layers of your soul to
> discover the mystery and magic that lies within. And join
> us as we gently, slowly, and safely guide you into a trance
> through a live shamanic DJ set so that your body will be
> ready for community energy workers to do their magic. This
> special event will take you on a journey through movement,
> dance, sound, breath, shamanic journeying, shape-shifting,
> trance-like states, and healing touch. We will be weaving
> magic from our own personal shamanic practices into an
> event unlike any other, an event to help you access the
> healing that already exists within you.[22]

Feigning an innocent spirituality, behind the advertisement is a cold plunge into demonic spirits and dark energy, drawing individuals further away from true light and into deeper darkness. Events such as these, which regularly make use of hallucinogenic teas or mushrooms, ceremonial cacao, or mescaline to induce altered states of consciousness, prey upon people's anxieties and personal insecurities, while promising healing and mystical encounters. Practices such as witchcraft and Wicca, relying "heavily on hedonism—sensual gratification and self-indulgence,"[23] encourage illicit drug use and deceive practitioners into welcoming demonic spirits, whereas Christianity teaches its followers to "be sober-minded," because "the devil is prowling around like a roaring lion, looking for anyone he can devour." Additionally, the Bible encourages "dying to self" and trusting in "[God's] power that is at work within us," rather than our own. In a Christian nation, contrasting Pagan practices with scriptural precepts may be sufficient to deter and dissuade the populace from participating in certain ungodly activities. However, in a post-Christian world that has firmly planted itself on the heretical terra firma of idolatry and witchcraft, such as contemporary America, this task is more challenging.

WITCHES IN THE CAMP

In a modern landscape where pop culture intertwines with ancient mysticism, celebrities like Ariana Grande have openly embraced occult practices, blurring the lines between entertainment and esoteric belief systems. In a revealing interview on the *Zach Sang Show*, Grande was asked, "Is there an in-between anywhere, where craft meets the universe?" The artist known by her fans as "Ari" answered, "Yeah, yeah, yeah. I'm somewhere in between, I've learned. I don't know, it's somewhere between being a literal witch, a literal witch, I'm not kidding. . . ."[24]

And it appears she isn't.

In her music video for the song "God is a Woman," Grande, who admits to carrying Queer tarot cards, "protecting dust," and rose quartz in her purse[25] (presumably as tools for spiritual insight and protection) showcases various elements of witchcraft and divine femininity. Throughout the video, Grande flaunts her mostly nude frame in several symbolic displays, including sitting enthroned within an occultic triangle, dancing within a celestial vortex as if begetting creation herself, and straddling the Earth in lingerie as a Gaia-like figure.[26]

Seemingly, behind Grande's esoteric spirituality is Kabbalah: a blend of Judaism and ancient mysticism. Grande is one of several celebrities to mix Kabbalistic concepts with New Age and occult practices. Although raised Catholic, Grande, whose brother is gay, admitted to *The Telegraph* that she distanced herself from the Christian faith after finding conflict with the Church's position on homosexuality. She confessed, "When my brother was told that God didn't love him I was like, 'OK, that's not cool.' They were building a Kabbalah center in Florida so we both checked it out and really had a connection with it."[27] Through the "tools" of Kabbalah, she added, "my life has unfolded in a really beautiful way."[28]

The influence of Kabbalah extends beyond Grande to other celebrities, like Britney Spears[29] and Madonna,[30] who have publicly endorsed its teachings and rituals, such as wearing the red string bracelet symbolizing initiation into this esoteric knowledge. Kabbalah, originally a secretive mystical practice among older men in Israel, has now permeated mainstream culture, enticing stars like Ashton Kutcher and ex-wife Demi Moore,[31] Gwyneth Paltrow,[32] and Paris Hilton.[33]

Joining Grande in her pursuit of witchcraft is Vanessa Hudgens, known for her roles in Disney films. Hudgens who openly identifies with witchcraft and has spoken about using tools like spirit boxes to communicate with dead spirits, recently described her practice:

> For me, it's kind of ritualistic. I do consider myself a witch and I love working with the moon and with herbs and with

stones and, you know, everything has a meaning and an
energy, and the more you learn about what everything has
to offer, the more you can use its energy to bring forth the
things you want in your life.[34]

In 2023, the star released a Discovery+ documentary, *Dead*
Hot: Season of the Witch, in which she delved into witchcraft,
ghost hunting, and connecting with the spirit world during her
journey in Salem, Massachusetts. A journey that she says started
at a young age, having spent her childhood chasing ghosts and
having mystical experiences with her childhood toys. Hudgens
reveals:

I've always been . . . very much an earth witch. I've always
felt the most grounded in nature . . . playing in the dirt and
. . . trying to make potions when I was, like, three years old,
that's always been something that has been a part of me,
but . . . now connecting to . . . my ancestors and my angels
and . . . just figuring out ways how to . . . ground myself . . .
spiritually; I feel it's just an empowering thing.[35]

While Hudgens doesn't define fully what she means, the term
"earth witch" usually describes someone who embraces spiritually misguided practices to harness power from the Earth's natural energies and cycles, contradicting the biblical view of God as
the sole source of true spiritual power. Instead of seeking guidance from the Creator, so-called Earth witches prioritize their
connection to nature above divine authority, often using herbs,
crystals, and rituals that are occultic or Pagan in nature. Drawn
in by the attractive exterior to witchcraft provided by faces like
Grande's and Hudgens, teens, and young adults, already indoctri-
nated by radical environmentalism and deeply concerned about

the health of the planet, become easy prey for Luciferian groomers and shaman practitioners who promote cosmic consciousness and revere earthly forces and elemental energy above the worship of the Almighty. As Paul writes in Romans, "They exchanged the truth of God for a lie and worshiped and served what has been created instead of the Creator."[36] This fascination with nature and the cosmos often leads these individuals to not just worship created things but to seek alternative creators altogether—creators that are out of this world.

ANCIENT ALIENS

In February 2024, Florida Congresswoman Anna Paulina Luna nearly broke the internet when she was asked about her investigation into a potential government coverup of unidentified anomalous phenomena, otherwise known as "UAPs." She answered, "I wouldn't call them aliens . . . I really like what [former U.S. Air Force intelligence officer David Grusch] calls them: He says that they're inter-dimensional beings, and he's very specific about that."[37]

Despite a robust 2024 U.S. Department of Defense investigation finding "no evidence that extraterrestrial intelligence has visited Earth or that authorities have recovered crashed alien spacecraft and are hiding them from the public,"[38] more than 51% of Americans still believe in extraterrestrials. Many are drawn to narratives suggesting that advanced alien civilizations imparted wisdom and technology to ancient humans, blending myth, science fiction, and spirituality into a belief system that replaces God with these alternative creators. This shift illustrates a deeper departure from traditional faith, as the allure of mystery and the unknown captivates those searching for meaning in an increasingly secular world.

One group expanding this search is METI International, who through the Goonhilly Satellite Earth Station in Cornwall, United Kingdom, beamed a message over 200 trillion miles into space to the Trappest-1 planetary system in October 2022, alerting any inter-dimensional beings who might be listening regarding the Earth's "climate crisis."[39] With a religious-like devotion to the organization's efforts, the President of METI International Douglas Vakoch offered, "Any aliens receiving our message won't be surprised to hear about our climate crisis. . . . They've had decades to observe our plight from afar."[40]

More than just a scientific exploration, Vakoch's comments demonstrate a blended ideology based on astronomy, radical environmentalism, and Pagan thought, where these space beings are either so advanced that they've been watching our planet for years, or they are omnisciently divine and worthy of worship. This better explains why, for the team at METI International, the search for extraterrestrial life holds a salvific role in society, whose adherents look to unconfirmed extraterrestrial beings in the heavens to rescue humanity from planetary destruction and provide ancient knowledge and technological advancements to propel humanity toward a utopic future.

Where groups such as METI International look toward future contact with extraterrestrials to save our planet, others, known as "ancient alien theorists," dive deeper into distorted thinking as they weave myth and archeology with a scriptural narrative, suggesting not only that these space beings might rescue us in the future but that they also laid the very foundations of our existence. Zecharia Sitchin, a popular ancient alien theorist, explains:

> I have done my best to show that there is no conflict
> between Bible and Science, Faith and Knowledge. The
> "Link" is missing, I said, because someone jumped the gun

on Evolution and used sophisticated genetic engineering to
upgrade a Homo erectus *or* Homo ergaster . . . *by mixing*
his genes with their advanced genes. That "someone" were
the biblical Elohim (whom the Sumerian called Anunnaki)
who came to Earth from their planet, Nibiru, fashioned The
Adam, then took the Daughters of Man as wives. That was
possible, I explained, because life on their planet and on our
planet is based on the same DNA.[41]

A now popular theory, Sitchin introduces the idea that a plurality of ancient beings, known as Anunnaki, Nephilim, or Elohim, came to Earth and created mankind by advancing our DNA from other early hominids, mated with the females of humans, and imparted unto their creation advanced knowledge. This theory, described as UFO spirituality, "is no longer comprised only of small cults; it's a burgeoning movement"[42] that is said to "fill the spiritual needs"[43] of an increasing cross-section of Americans who seek to find a way to harmonize their radical views of the environment with a higher form of spirituality. Additionally, since the worship of alien beings doesn't have a central text, such as the Bible, there is no single truth. The quest for the Anunnaki, thus, represents a form of informal spirituality that values individuality, free from the need to adhere to established moral standards or core principles. This doesn't prevent its followers, though, from hijacking passages of scripture to justify their idolatrous position:

When mankind began to multiply on the earth and
daughters were born to them, the sons of God saw that the
daughters of mankind were beautiful, and they took any they
chose as wives for themselves. And the Lord said, "My Spirit
will not remain with mankind forever, because they are

corrupt. Their days will be 120 years." The Nephilim were on the earth both in those days and afterward, when the sons of God came to the daughters of mankind, who bore children to them. They were the powerful men of old, the famous men.[44]

The historical view of Genesis 6 presents divergent interpretations that profoundly influence one's understanding of the biblical narrative. Embracing biblical orthodoxy, Christians typically regard the Nephilim as spiritual beings or fallen angels, seeing them as a manifestation of spiritual corruption and rebellion against God's design for humanity. In contrast, interpretations that label the Nephilim as ancient aliens diminish the theological significance of these passages, substituting divine judgment and spiritual warfare with speculative theories that deviate from foundational Christian teachings about the nature of God, humanity, and redemption. In this view, it isn't Christ who will return to earth, but ancient extraterrestrials. As Erich von Däniken writes, "I know definitively that Earth, our home, has been visited by extraterrestrials in the distant past. I also know that those visitors promised our forebears they will return to earth. They will return—so humanity had better come to grips with that thought." These views start to make more sense of Luna's term "interdimensional beings," which better explains their true identity— fallen angels!

In ancient times the greatest seduction into idolatry was to worship the sun, moon, and stars. Because these celestial bodies dominated the sky it was an easy sell for a cult leader. The Nephilim (called the Anunnaki in Mesopotamia) said they were from the stars. These early deceptions paved the way for today's ancient astronaut theorists who believe man was created by aliens. There is a growing cult that is looking for a New Age savior to come as an alien.[45]

Alien seekers, by venerating these cosmic spirits and other-worldly guides, are opening a portal into their hearts and minds for fallen angels and demonic beings to divert their attention from the worship of the true Creator, Yahweh, the God of the Bible, and toward a complex web of deception and false doctrines. By turning to these alternative beliefs, UFO spiritualists embrace a worldview that maligns biblical teaching and promotes a form of New Age Pagan idolatry. They are drawn to these ideas by a quest for harmony and higher knowledge, seeking a spiritual connection, that isn't Christianity, that they perceive as transcending earthly limitations. According to A.M. Gittlitz's summary of J. Posadas, an Argentine Trotskyist who advocated for nuclear war as a means to end capitalism,[46] in order to have any hope of overcoming war and class struggle, humanity must look to these interstellar travelers to usher in a truly socialist society:

> For alien civilizations to travel hundreds of light years to Earth, he wrote, they would need to have an "infinitely superior" form of social organization, "without struggle and antagonisms." Marxists call the type of society that has advanced beyond our current divisions of nation, class, race, and gender—a society in which each gives according to their ability and takes according to their needs—socialist.[47]

Ignoring the numerous disastrously failed attempts over the past 100 years to implement socialism throughout the world, Pagan dreamers, like J. Posadas, would rather continue their fool's errand of chasing a global utopian homeostasis courtesy of insidious space demons than acknowledge their rebellious attitude toward God and accept the transformative hope and redemption offered through faith in Jesus Christ. Instead, they persist deeper in their pursuit of Pagan and Marxist pablum, driven by a quest for balance encapsulated in the Pagan symbol of the yin and yang.

YIN AND YANG

One common denominator among radical environmentalists, Pagan occultists, and UFO spiritualists is their shared sense of an approaching global cataclysmic event. Atheistic scientists warn of "errant asteroids, soaring superflares, and exploding super-novae,"[48] as well as threats of food shortages, contaminated water, and the impact of "when cows belch and fart."[49] More esoteric Pagans speak of the death of the gods in the battle of Ragnarok,[50] the Q'ero Inca Shamans' idea of Pachacuti, or earth-shaking.[51] UFO spiritualists, meanwhile, fear the disruption of cosmic harmony or the consequences of interstellar conflict. But more often than not, this diverse godless spectrum between mystic and scientific collides into an alchemical belief system driven by Leftist scientific propaganda and Luciferian religion. The glue, of course, that holds them all together is Marxist ideology.

The result is fear, panic, and a "sky-is-falling" mindset, that if not willingly reciprocated by those around them, leads to forced mandates and green policies designed to control the masses. In this repressive framework, individuals are free to believe anything they want to believe, assuming it isn't Christianity. The reason for this is that Christianity, with its emphasis on moral absolutes and spiritual truths, stands in contrast to the relativistic and materialistic worldview promoted by Marxist ideology and embraced by many radical environmentalists and worshipers of earth and space. Whereas Christianity holds that eternal salvation is only found in Christ and that our present world is destined for destruction,[52] Pagan practices, such as shamanism, witchcraft, or ancient alien theory, pumped full of Marxist dogma, seek to establish a new order based on perceived ecological and social justice, striving for a balance that aligns with their vision of a harmonious existence—an unattainable utopian planet Earth.

Within this framework, there is a tendency to view humanity as inherently disruptive to this balance, likening it to a virus, necessitating stringent regulations, such as onerous emissions standards[53] or state-wide bans on gas stoves,[54] and societal reorganization to mitigate perceived environmental harm, like minimizing meat consumption[55] or restricting the use of personal vehicles.[56] Guided by the Hegelian idea of progress through conflict, a yin-yang dynamic develops among Pagans in power, through which two opposing forces become complementary and, in their minds, necessary for cosmic harmony.

These forces don't simply complement one another, but they transform and flow into one another in an endless cycle. To understand this properly, consider Medium contributor Kenan Kolday's explanation:

> *The yin yang also shows that within each thing there is the seed of its opposite. For instance, a snowflake has the potential to become a drop of water which has the potential to become steam which the potential to become a cloud. Nothing is ever completely yin or yang, but rather a mixture of both in varying degrees.*[57]

From a neo-Pagan perspective, this means that light contains darkness, and darkness contains light. War contains peace, and peace contains war. Standing as a blatant rejection of biblical truth, the concept of the yin and yang defiantly disregards the testimony of John's first letter:

> *This is the message we have heard from him and declare to you: God is light, and there is absolutely no darkness in him. If we say, "We have fellowship with him," and yet we walk in darkness, we are lying and are not practicing the truth.*

If we walk in the light as he himself is in the light, we have
fellowship with one another, and the blood of Jesus his Son
cleanses us from all sin.[58]

As John declares, in the light of God, there is no darkness, and those who dwell in darkness have no fellowship with the light. Dismissing this truth, Pagan practitioners and Woke ideologues embrace a worldview that twists and distorts fundamental realities, like holiness, righteousness, and justice. In their attempt to blend and reconcile opposites like yin and yang, they create a false dichotomy that rejects the absolute nature of divine truth. This flawed perspective not only undermines the clear distinctions between light and darkness, good and evil, but also contributes to a broader cultural confusion about identity and morality.

For those who adhere to a radical left Pagan worldview, this confusion reaches its zenith in the full expression of the yin and yang principle, manifesting in a profound denial of the immutable truths revealed in Christianity, and vividly embodied in the shifting, ambiguous constructs of today's most sinister form of witchcraft: Transgenderism. This new twisted element preposterously concludes that the male can exist within the female, and the female can exist within the male. Through this, these modern witches cast their strongest spell, deluding humanity into believing they can become whatever they desire, no matter how perverted and crude.

FOUR

TRANSGENDERISM AND THE OCCULT

SOCIAL CONTAGIONS AND IDEOLOGICAL COLONIZATION

Revealing the cascading and deleterious spread of gender theory in America, a recent study published in *General Psychiatry* by Dr. Ching-Fang Sun of Virginia Tech Carilion School of Medicine, demonstrated a substantial increase in gender dysphoria diagnoses between 2017 and 2021, especially among young females.[1] Unpacking his findings, Sun elucidated, "Our study demonstrated a climbing prevalence of gender dysphoria especially in those assigned female at birth."*[2] Despite his politically correct language, Sun deciphered what we all know— gender theory increasingly targets children, especially young girls, and creates irreparable damage in their lives. While most of us are aware of this troubling trend, what may be less recognized is that the underlying ideology driving it has roots in Pagan beliefs and practices perpetuated by social pressures and intentional ideological campaigns.

Walt Heyer, a gender dysphoria expert and founder of Sex Change Regret, spoke to this deadly pattern and called

---

* *Note:* The term "assigned female at birth" is used here to align with contemporary terminology in gender studies. From a Christian perspective, the author believes that sex is determined by God at conception and is not subject to human assignment.

transgenderism a "social contagion" in a 2019 interview with Legatus. He elaborated:

> *If we put this into a context where we're talking about kids, we know kids go through identity issues in many different ways over a period of time. We're now in a cycle where this social contagion of transgenderism is taking place, but it's really young individuals who are opting for this. These are usually people who aren't really good at social adaptability and this is sort of an instant way for them to steal the attention that they don't get or wouldn't have gotten as who they really are.*

Heyer, who himself underwent gender reassignment surgery and lived eight years as a "transgender woman" before finding Christ and detransitioning in the early 1990s, has since used his story to expose the dangers of so-called "gender-affirming care." However, there is a key distinction between Heyer's experience and the current wave of young people caught in the riptide of gender theory: Heyer, now 84, was born before the advent of social media and widespread gender therapy.

Retelling his experience, Heyer shared with *USA Today*:

> *I started my transgender journey as a four-year-old boy when my grandmother repeatedly, over several years, cross-dressed me in a full-length purple dress she made especially for me and told me how pretty I was as a girl. This planted the seed of gender confusion and led to my transitioning at age 42 to transgender female.*[3]

For Heyer, neglect, abuse, and childhood trauma set him on a destructive path of gender confusion. While young people today may also experience trauma, what's novel is the pervasive influence of social contagion and ideological manipulation, which are now fueling and accelerating the movement toward gender dysphoria among today's youth. In fact, a recent study from the CDC found that 3% of high school students "self-identify as transgender," despite only 0.1% of teens receiving gender-related medicines.[4] While trauma may serve as the entry point for gender dysphoria in a small number of young people, it is the societal contagions and ideological forces that are now propelling them further down this destructive path—and the consequences are profoundly harmful.

According to one study, "the number of people seeking gender-affirming surgeries, such as breast and chest operations or genital reconstruction, nearly tripled during the three years before the coronavirus pandemic."[5] This alarming statistic does not even account for the thousands of individuals, including children, who have undergone morally reprehensible treatments like puberty blockers and cross-sex hormone therapy, which often cause irreparable damage, including sterilization and long-lasting emotional trauma.

While many European nations, like Finland, Sweden, and the Netherlands,[6] are instilling stricter guidelines, and in some cases bans, on puberty blockers, cross-sex hormones, and sex reassignment surgeries—similar to the one passed by Russia's lower house of parliament in 2023[7]—U.S.-based organizations such as the Human Rights Campaign push for fewer regulations, claiming, despite the evidence to the contrary,[8] that gender-affirming care is "safe," "fully reversible," and "life-saving."[9]

Behind the curtain of gender theory and manipulating the social contagion aspects of the transgender movement, lies what Pope Francis referred to as a form of "ideological colonization."[10] By ideological colonization, Pope Francis likely was warning against attempts of wealthy countries and organizations "to link development aid to the acceptance of social policies such as those allowing gay marriage and contraception." For example, in 2024, the Biden-Harris administration awarded over $5 million in aid to U.S.-based organizations that conduct "family counseling and support for lesbian, gay, bisexual, transgender, queer/questioning, intersex+ youth and their families." Recipients included the University of Arizona, Boston-based The Home for Little Wanderers, Inc., and Arbor Circle Corporation of Grand Rapids, Michigan.[11]

While financial support such as this is being used to fund trans-friendly organizations, it's also being used to defund and punish nations and organizations that refuse to align themselves with the dogmas of the global gender cult. In 2023, then-President Joe Biden, who boasted that his administration was "making equality the centerpiece of our diplomacy around the world," imposed visa restrictions and paused approximately $15 million in aid,[12] in what appeared to be direct retaliation of Uganda's Christian-inspired strong stance against homosexuality, even though many of our Middle Eastern allies have much stricter anti-gay laws in place.

Zeroing in on the main point and helping to make sense of the real motives behind trans-related ideological colonization, John Daniel Davidson, senior editor at *The Federalist* and author of *Pagan America: The Decline of Christianity and the Dark Age to Come*, offers:

> *One plausible explanation is that the trans movement is not, despite the insistence of its champions, a civil rights struggle for equality and dignity. Nor is it a struggle for access to necessary health care. Nor, for that matter, is it really a political movement. It is, in fact, a Pagan religious*

movement, the tenets of which include the idea that
some people are born in the wrong body and that a man
can become a woman, or vice versa, simply by willing it
so. Abigail Shrier has argued that gender ideology is a
"fundamentalist religion—intolerant, demanding strict
adherence to doctrine, hell-bent on gathering proselytes," and
that gender identity is "the secular version of the soul."[13]

Hiding behind foreign policy and health care claims, as both Davidson and Shrier accurately acknowledge, is the real agenda—a spiritual motivation driving the mass conversion of a legion of alphabet-worshiping converts. Davidson identifies the Pagan rationale shaping this motivation as a belief in the "misalignment of body and soul,"[14] in which somehow either God or nature messed up, and as a result, we must ascend to the place of God to do what He apparently could not. While this is certainly part of it, Davidson, who rightly acknowledges the "confused tangle of contradictions"[15] within gender theory, seems to inadvertently attribute to the trans movement an actual objective reality regarding which soul should reside in a given body—as if there were a genuine moral or scientific issue to resolve. What remain to be explored, though, are the twisted dualistic (male and female) Pagan beliefs underlying this ideological movement, which have no basis in science or morality but are rooted in esoteric and occult thought.

JESUS AND DIONYSUS

In July 2024, approximately two weeks after the first attempted assassination of President Donald Trump in Butler, Pennsylvania, the world erupted again as the opening ceremony of the Olympic

Games in Paris blurred the lines between Leonardi DaVinci's depiction of the *Last Supper* and the *Feast of Dionysus*. At the center of the long table display was LGBTQ+ activist and drag performer Barbara Butch, who was surrounded by 17 other half-dressed drag and transgendered performers, including one male performer who had his scrotum protruding from the side of his shorts.[16] The performance, widely denounced by religious leaders, sparked debate among the public over whether it was a satirical take on DaVinci's portrayal of Christ's Last Supper with His disciples before the crucifixion or a representation of the Pagan feast of Dionysus, the Greek god tied to wine, fertility, and celebration.

The perverted performance, which according to one Olympic spokesperson "took inspiration from Leonardo da Vinci's famous painting to create the setting," is a perfect example of a motte-and-bailey fallacy in which "an arguer conflates two positions that share similarities, one modest and easy to defend (the 'motte') and one much more controversial and harder to defend (the 'bailey')."[17] For Woke activists, this tactic is used to slowly advance radical ideological positions while simultaneously claiming that the ideas are completely harmless. Using this ploy, the Olympic opening ceremony, which reeked of Paganism, sexual debauchery, and anti-Christ sentiments, was allowed to occur under the seemingly innocent guise that it wasn't meant to offend anyone, but only "highlight diversity and inclusion."[18] As a tactic, this often deflects accusations from critics by shifting the focus from the radical position to the more socially accepted ideological framework, thus making the accuser appear problematic.

In this case, the tactic wasn't perfectly executed, though, as the motte—an appeal to diversity and inclusion and the idea that all are welcome at the table—was much harder to defend by the performers and Olympic spokespersons. Whether the performance was intended as a parody of *The Last Supper* or a re-enactment of the *Feast of Dionysus*, it was still inappropriate, as it was riddled with excessive, disgusting, and nearly pornographic imagery.

However, the more radical objective—the bailey—that was obscured amidst the controversy over its religious offense and disturbing Pagan symbols is that the performance highlighted a central aspect of Pagan ideology: the integration of transgender themes. This critical element was lost in the debate, which fixated on whether the depiction was of Jesus or Dionysus, or intentionally meant to offend believers.

Focusing solely on whether the performance was a parody of Jesus or a deliberate offense to Christians overlooks a more profound issue. The inclusion of transgender themes in the performance, as we will explore, reveals a deeper, more malignant layer of spiritual deception. This incorporation of transgender elements aligns with an ancient Pagan depiction of the devil as a being who embodies both male and female attributes. To fully understand the Pagan threat in our nation, we must first uncover why radical Marxists, Pagans, and LGBTQ+ activists are so fixated on the dualistic concept of gender.

DIVINE HERMAPHRODITE

"Womanhood, to the non-theosophical thinker, must ever remain an enigma," penned Susan E. Gay in 1890 for *Lucifer* magazine in an article entitled "The Future of Woman." Long before Sen. Marsha Blackburn asked U.S. Supreme Court Justice Ketanji Brown Jackson, during her confirmation hearings in March 2022, to define what a woman is,[19] theosophist writers, like Gay and Blavatsky, were exploring what they felt were the inexplicable aspects of womanhood. According to Gay, the feminine gender is so complex that a "non-theosophical thinker" can't comprehend it. She explains that:

> Only in the light of re-embodiment is it possible to understand the question of sex fully, or, we might say, even at all. What, then, appears to the outer perception to be a woman is simply a soul temporarily clothed in the garb of womanhood, the experiences of which have been earned by it, or are essential to its further development. The "sin" of physical marriage certainly does not originate souls and immortality. And even the bodily form owes its origin to a past dating far beyond all our present knowledge of history and a past in which sex expressed itself under wholly different aspects from those we know. Here, at last, we begin to understand somewhat of human life, and its varied conditions. There has, in truth, never been any distinctly marked line between the sexes, or, rather, to put it in other words, many men are to be found in the ranks of women, and many women in the ranks of men. They are there for their own discipline rather than anything else.[20]

For Gay, biological sex, or what she calls the "outer perception" of a physical body, doesn't necessarily correlate to the gender identity of the soul. According to theosophy, this is due to "re-embodiment," in which they believe the soul migrates throughout many lifetimes and multiple bodies, both male and female, as part of its spiritual evolution or enlightenment. Thus, a feminine soul could live in a masculine body and vice versa. Influenced by theosophical ideology, modern Woke warriors lean into this strange metaphysical phenomenon, made popular by thinkers like Gay and Blavatsky, to justify separating biological sex from gender identity.

Understanding the Pagan and cult-inspired beliefs behind the "enigma" of gender identity, it is easier to understand why individuals, such as Justice Jackson, are unable to define the term. They aren't being coy—they are being cultish.

And so, we find that the confusion over gender is no accident. What many interpret as intellectual complexity or cultural progress is an ancient rebellion from the Father of Lies that has sought to distort God's design for creation. The notion that biological sex and gender identity can be separated is not some New Age philosophical breakthrough; it's a resurrection of the Pagan belief that the natural order can be bent and reshaped to fit human desires. This isn't just an intellectual trend—it's the work of spiritual forces that seek to sever humanity from the truth of who we are meant to be. Said another way, it's a doctrine of demons instituted by Satan himself.

HERMAPHRODITE LUCIFER

Traditionally, Christian thinkers such as St. Augustine, Origen, and Thomas Aquinas, have taught that angels and demons possess "no composition of matter and form,"[21] meaning they exist in a spiritual dimension and are without a physical body. While most have assumed that beings lacking a body imply that they are without gender, it's important to note that scripture only uses the masculine gender to refer to angels or demons. Likewise, the devil is also only referred to in the Bible in the masculine form, as displayed in the following examples:

- "One day the sons of God came again to present themselves before the Lord, and Satan also came with them to present himself before the Lord."
  —Job 2:1 (CSB)

- "If Satan drives out Satan, he is divided against himself. How then will his kingdom stand?"
  —Matthew 12:26 (CSB)
- "If Satan also is divided against himself, how will his kingdom stand? For you say I drive out demons by Beelzebul."
  —Luke 11:18 (CSB)
- "And no wonder! For Satan disguises himself as an angel of light."
  —2 Corinthians 11:14 (CSB)
- "So the great dragon was thrown out—the ancient serpent, who is called the devil and Satan, the one who deceives the whole world. He was thrown to earth, and his angels with him."
  —Revelation 12:9 (CSB)

Ignoring theological tradition and scriptural references, a concept emerged in the Middle Ages within esoteric and Pagan religious systems, emphasizing themes of duality, androgyny, and the unity of opposites such as male and female. This led to the portrayal of Lucifer or Satan in a hermaphroditic manner. Drawing upon Greek mythology's Hermaphroditus—a deity with both male and female attributes—these depictions of a Hermaphrodite Lucifer appeared in various writings, paintings, and occult symbolism.

One of the most infamous representations of the hermaphroditic Lucifer is known as Baphomet. The term "Baphomet" first appeared in historical texts as early as 1098, mentioned by Anselm of Ribemont in a letter describing the Siege of Antioch during the First Crusade.[22] Initially believed to refer to "an alteration of 'Mahomet,' or Muhammad, the founder of Islam,"[23] the term evolved within esoteric traditions to symbolize duality and androgyny. The most influential depiction of Baphomet, however, is attributed to Eliphas Lévi, a French occultist, who vividly illustrated the figure in his 1854 work *Dogme et Rituel de la Haute Magie* (Dogma and Ritual of High Magic). Lévi's Baphomet, characterized by a goat-headed creature with a blend of male and female features, including female breasts and a symbolic male sex organ, became a prominent symbol in occult and esoteric Pagan practices. Lévi, according to Per Faxneld, "popularized the word occultism . . . and his books were instrumental in bringing about the 'occult revival' of the mid-and late 19th century."[24] Like many occultic figures, Lévi was influenced by "socialist and feminist politics."[25] His engravings and writings arguably deeply shaped his ideological successors, such as Blavatsky and Aleister Crowley,[26] the English occultist and founder of Thelema. While his depiction of Baphomet is arguably the most recognizable, depictions of the hermaphroditic Lucifer can be found much earlier than his work.

Faxneld explains that, "visual representations of the Devil did not become common until the ninth century,"[27] and that in these portrayals "Satan quite often exhibits some female anatomical parts, typically breasts."[28] This artistic phenomenon, which Faxneld calls "gender-bending,"[29] appears in artwork throughout the Medieval and Renaissance periods,[30] appearing alongside the occultic practices that stemmed from this period, including alchemy, astrology, and Kabbalah. However, none of these esoteric ideas have shaped gender theory, androgyny, and the trans movement more than the rediscovery of Hermeticism.

DUALISM AND THE OCCULT

In the decades following the life of Christ, a new syncretistic philosophical and religious system emerged known as "Hermeticism."

Constructed from "Hellenistic philosophy . . . interspersed with motifs from Egyptian mythology and themes of Jewish and Iranian origin,"[31] Hermeticism is based upon the pseudepigraphical writings of a mythical figure named Hermes Trismegistus. Part philosopher, prophet, and Pagan god, Hermes Trismegistus, as described by Ebeling, was an amalgamation of the Egyptian god Thoth and the Hellenistic deity Hermes:[32]

In Hellenistic Egypt, Hermes Trismegistus arose from a merging of the figures of Thoth and Hermes. After the conquest of Egypt by Alexander the Great in the year 332 B.C.E., the Greeks in Egypt adopted the outward forms of Egyptian culture, investing them, however, with their own Greek content. In the interpretatio graeca, foreign deities, including those of Egypt, were understood as equivalents of Greek gods and goddesses; they were different in form but identical in essence. By that time, however, deities of different cultures had already been identified with one another. In the fifth century, Herodotus wrote that Hermes and Thoth corresponded to each other, for both were considered to be tricksters, and sometimes even thieves, who, equipped with magical capabilities, were messengers of the gods and conductors of the dead. This new Hermes, this Hermes-Thoth, was more than the sum of his parts, however. He took on a new life, and from the second century on was graced with the epithet Trismegistus, the "thrice great."[33]

Initial variations of Hermeticism found safe harbor among mystics and intellectuals, Neoplatonists, as well as Gnostic Christians, where it stood as a type of "third position between Christianity and Paganism,"[34] but the practice was eventually condemned by patristic Church fathers, including St. Augustine of

Hippo, who devoted several chapters in his classic work *The City of God*, dismantling Hermes' writings before calling him "a friend ... of demons," who "does not clearly express the name of Christ."[35] Even with Augustine's stringent condemnation of Hermeticism, the tradition never fully died out and it has remained "one of the undercurrents of Western cultural memory." While the writings of Hermes Trismegistus may be largely foreign to modern individuals, notwithstanding philosophers and occult practitioners, the core tenets of Hermetic thought are far from obsolete. In fact, many of these ancient principles have seeped into the groundwater of contemporary Woke ideology and are profoundly influencing everything from gender theory to cancel culture.

Dr. James Lindsay, coauthor of *The Queering of the American Child: How a New School Religious Cult Poisons the Minds and Bodies of Normal Kids*, explained in a 2022 lecture at the Mere Simulacrity conference in Phoenix, Arizona, how "Hermetic alchemical magic,"[36] mixed with Gnosticism, has become the mechanism driving what he calls "the Secret Religions of the West," after post-Renaissance thinkers, such as Hegel and Marx rediscovered Hermeticism.

> *What Hegel actually did was take Gnosticism and Hermeticism and hammered them together into one ... coherent, systematic thing he called a philosophy, or in fact a science, and because Hermeticism believes that all religions are a reflection of the one secret true religion ... so he hammered Gnosticism and Hermeticism into Christianity and called it science. Marx flipped that over, which you can say made it satanic ... turned it very Gnostic, which you could also say is satanic ... and called ... the result "scientific socialism."*[37]

Hegel, as Lindsay elaborates, merged Gnosticism and Hermeticism into a systematic framework he termed a "science." This new science, rooted in the teachings of Hermes Trismegistus and the texts attributed to him, such as *The Corpus Hermeticum* and *The Emerald Tablet*, is built upon the axiom: "that which is above is from that which is below, and that which is below is from that which is above, working the miracles of one."[38] In simpler terms, "As above, so below; as below, so above."[39] This principle, which Lindsay likens to a snake eating its own tail, is central to Hermeticism. For the Hermeticist, this axiom "seeks to infuse all human endeavor with sacredness—to align all human activity with the Divine Will."[40] While this tenet was present before Hegel's work, the collective efforts of Hegel and Marx transposed Hermeticism from an individual esoteric tradition to a collective satanic cult, in which *all* human activity *must* align with the new mystical science.

Consider the Indiana couple who had their child removed from their home by the courts after refusing to use "feminine pronouns to identify their son, who demanded to be called by a female name after he told his parents in 2019 that he identified as a girl."[41] Or the case of Jeannette Cooper, a Chicago mother who lost her parental rights after refusing to call her 12-year-old daughter, who "suddenly claimed to be transgender,"[42] a boy. Tragically, these stories serve as examples of how the trans movement, fueled by "scientific socialism," creates forced acceptance of preferred gender pronouns (PGPs) and gender identities. The reasoning goes something like this:

- ALL human endeavor is sacred.
- Trans identity is a type of human endeavor and is therefore sacred.
- Therefore, ALL human activity must align with trans identity.

- Those who refuse to align with the sacredness of trans identity must be forced to align.

In this way, Hermeticism, while not originally designed as a tool of totalitarianism now hijacked by Marxist elites, provides ideological and spiritual justification for dismantling traditional moral values by imposing socialist tactics and cult-like pseudoscientific reasoning on the general populace. This makes Hermeticism particularly effective at blurring moral distinctions and obscuring the truth. Its core tenets, known as the Seven Hermetic Principles, bear a superficial resemblance to Christian values, leading to their misinterpretation as orthodoxy while simultaneously distorting views of truth and the natural order. While based on ancient writings, the Seven Hermetic Principles are a modern formulation, mostly derived from The Kybalion, a twentieth-century work written by three individuals who went by the collective pseudonym The Three Initiates. Instilled with the echoes of ancient alchemy, including the belief that "everything in the organic world manifests both genders,"[43] the principles listed below have silently ravaged the modern world and weaponized a generation of Marxist activists against the foundations of reason, morality, and divinity—especially in the realm of gender and sexuality:

The Seven Hermetic Principles

1. *The Principle of Mentalism.* The idea that "The All Is Mind" suggests that reality is a mental construct. This principle has been twisted to support the notion that gender is purely a mental and subjective experience, detached from biological reality, thus fueling the belief that one can choose or change their gender identity based on personal feelings.

2. *The Principle of Correspondence.* "As above, so below; as below, so above." This principle implies a direct correspondence between different planes of existence. In the context of gender theory, it has been misused to argue that the internal sense of gender identity (the mental) should correspond with the external expression of that identity, leading to the normalization of gender fluidity and the rejection of traditional gender norms.

3. *The Principle of Vibration.* "Nothing rests; everything moves; everything vibrates." This principle is often cited to justify the idea that gender is fluid and constantly in flux, reinforcing the belief that one's gender identity can change over time and is not fixed.

4. *The Principle of Polarity.* "Everything is dual; everything has poles; everything has its pair of opposites." While this principle traditionally refers to the dual nature of reality, it has been co-opted to argue that gender exists on a spectrum, with male and female being mere extremes, allowing for the existence of various non-binary and gender-fluid identities.

5. *The Principle of Rhythm.* "Everything flows, out and in; everything has its tides; all things rise and fall." This principle has been used to suggest that gender identity can ebb and flow, leading to the acceptance of non-binary identities and the idea that one's gender can shift over time, rather than being a stable and unchanging aspect of identity.

6. *The Principle of Cause and Effect.* "Every cause has its effect; every effect has its cause." In the realm of gender theory, this principle is sometimes invoked to justify the belief that societal pressures and cultural narratives cause individuals to question and ultimately alter their gender

identities, reinforcing the notion that gender is socially constructed rather than biologically determined.

7. *The Principle of Gender.* "Gender is in everything; everything has its Masculine and Feminine Principles." This principle has been distorted to promote the idea that every individual contains both masculine and feminine energies, thus validating gender fluidity and the belief that one can embody or express different genders at different times, contributing to the widespread acceptance of transgenderism and non-binary identities.

While the focus here is on gender identity and sexual orientation, similar applications of the Hermetic tradition are employed by occultic Marxists to advance Leftist agendas related to environmentalism, race, globalism, and more. What truly matters is the recognition that the global Woke cult is using these Hermetic principles to justify a Leftist agenda and to ascend into gods themselves. This is not just a political movement; it is a philosophical and religious idea that is driving the current political worldview. According to *The Corpus Hermeticum*, it is "through the sciences and arts"[44] that man emanates his deity, becoming "higher than the gods"[45] and achieving gnosis. According to Hermes Trismegistus, the process involves "an intercourse of souls,"[46] in which God, who is described as "being male and female,"[47] intertwines with both the Cosmos (creation) and man, wherein the "Cosmos is subject, then, to God, man to the Cosmos . . . but God is o'er them all, and God contains them all. God's rays, to use a figure, are His energies; the Cosmos's are natures, the arts and sciences are man's."[48] Later, the writer adds that through this "intellectual birth . . . we are made into Gods."[49]

These principles, repackaged for modern consumption, have stealthily infiltrated societal structures, encouraging a worldview that is deceptively close to orthodox belief but fundamentally opposed to the truth. This distorted spirituality, now wielded as a weapon by those seeking to upend traditional values, has become a key tool in the Marxist strategy to destabilize society and impose a new order by redefining the very essence of humanity itself, opening the next frontier in this ideological battle—directed evolution.

DIRECTED EVOLUTION

"We believe it will get to the stage where we can sit down at a computer and design the organism we want just by ordering in the parts,"[50] forecasted Clyde Hutchison, a pioneer in the field of synthetic biology. Hutchison, via his lab at the University of North Carolina, is working to decode the essential building blocks of life by manipulating bacteria and "harmless" viruses. Hutchison, who said "I don't think there's anything wrong with playing God,"[51] is just one of many genetic experts, environmental scientists, and molecular biologists who are relentlessly pushing to reshape the world according to their own agendas, often disregarding ethical boundaries and the potential consequences of their actions.

In the past, such scientific discoveries were often hailed as a triumph of human intellect and progress. However, the COVID-19 pandemic revealed a darker side to these advancements. It became evident how easily science could be manipulated and weaponized to justify and enforce tyrannical laws and policies. The same technologies, once praised for their potential to improve lives, were suddenly tools of control used to limit freedoms and impose unprecedented restrictions on society. This shift in perspective has exposed the true motives often guiding such scientific endeavors and the unchecked power they may grant to those in authority.

Here are some discoveries and advancements that could be construed as tools for control or manipulation:

- *CRISPR Gene Editing.* Initially celebrated for its potential to cure genetic diseases, CRISPR technology also raises ethical concerns about human genetic modification and the potential for "designer babies."
- *Artificial Intelligence in Surveillance.* AI advancements in facial recognition and data tracking, once hailed for their security benefits, have sparked fears of mass surveillance and invasion of privacy.
- *Synthetic Biology.* The creation of synthetic organisms, like those pioneered by Hutchison, can lead to unforeseen consequences, including ecological disruption or the development of new biological weapons.[52]
- *Digital Health Passports.* Introduced during the COVID-19 pandemic, digital health passports became a way to control movement and enforce compliance with health mandates, raising massive concerns about privacy and personal freedom.[53]
- *Gain-of-Function Research.* The alteration of pathogens to study their potential impact came under intense scrutiny during the COVID-19 pandemic. Dr. Anthony Fauci and others were linked to funding such research, raising concerns about the origins of the virus and the potential for manipulated organisms to cause global crises, especially when shrouded in secrecy and lacking proper oversight.[54]
- *Solar Sun Shades.* Proposed as a geoengineering solution to combat climate change, solar sun shades aim to reflect sunlight away from the Earth to reduce global temperatures. While touted as a potential fix for so-called global warming, this technology has raised significant

concerns about unintended consequences, such as disrupting weather patterns and ecosystems. Moreover, the ability to control the planet's climate could become a powerful tool for those seeking to manipulate global conditions for political or economic gain, leading to fears of environmental tyranny.[55]

Driving many of these discoveries is a Hermetic-Marxist god-complex manifesting in directed evolution—an intentional manipulation of God's created order to reimagine a better world than the one we have been given. Rather than accepting the limitations and ethical boundaries inherent in our natural world, these scientists and technologists often pursue their ambitions with little regard for the broader implications. A fusion of science and spirituality, directed evolution is a radical extension of Hermetic principles aimed at manipulating gender, biology, and genetic engineering. This approach reflects a Hermetic-Marxist agenda that seeks to reshape mankind in the image of a new esoteric order, fundamentally altering what it means to be human. If a man can become a woman, and a young boy can transform into a cat, then a robot can become a man, and a man can become a robot. Directed evolution mimics natural selection but with a critical difference: Rather than nature or God, man decides the outcome.

To be clear, the problem isn't medical advancement or scientific discovery, it's godlessness. When there is no consideration of our Creator, and morals are absent, progress will always lead us astray. From a Christian vantage point, true progress aims to conform us to the image of Christ.

As such, progress should always:

- Recognize God as our Creator.
- Acknowledge that man is not God.

- Be based upon God's created order.
- Refrain from acting as God upon the earth (i.e., deciding who lives or who dies).

In this context, transgenderism and trans surgeries are forms of directed evolution that exemplify the problems inherent in a godless approach to scientific and medical advancements. By rejecting the immutable aspects of biological sex and pursuing gender transitions, these practices reflect a radical departure from God's created order. Such surgeries and treatments are based on the belief that one's gender identity can override the biological reality of sex, an idea that aligns with the Hermetic-Marxist agenda of manipulating human nature. This not only disregards the ethical implications of altering God's design but also raises concerns about the long-term psychological and physical effects on individuals. From a Christian perspective, these practices are seen as attempts to redefine human identity in ways that conflict with the divine blueprint, ultimately leading us away from the true image of Christ and the moral truths outlined in Scripture.

EMERGING GLOBAL TYRANNY

As the Hermetic-Marxist agenda increasingly shapes our societal landscape, it becomes evident that these ideologies are not merely philosophical but are actively influencing global governance and policy-making. The elites driving this agenda are leveraging their positions of power to impose a new order that aligns with their esoteric and totalitarian vision. This emerging global tyranny, cloaked in the guise of progressive reform and scientific advancement, seeks to transform not just societal structures but the very essence of human nature itself.

The seamless integration of Hermetic principles into contemporary policy underscores a deeper, more troubling reality. Pagan spiritual enlightenment is being weaponized to justify sweeping changes that fundamentally alter our understanding of identity, morality, and governance. By merging the core tenets of Hermeticism with Marxist doctrines, these elites are crafting a narrative that elevates their own power while undermining traditional values and Christian convictions. This shift is evident in the growing influence of transhumanist and technocratic ideologies, which prioritize human augmentation and social engineering over divine order and ethical constraints.

While this chapter has explored the historical roots and occult influences shaping the present technocratic movement, understanding these origins is only part of the battle. To effectively counter the looming global tyranny, it is crucial to identify and confront the elites constructing this theosophical Tower of Babel. These figures are not just shadowy actors but powerful influencers leading organizations whose agendas are driving the redefinition of human identity and representative governance. In the next section, we will uncover these key players' identities, motivations, and strategies, revealing how their neo-Pagan ambitions are shaping a new world order that threatens our freedoms and moral values. The true challenge lies in exposing and challenging their vision for the future—a vision that could redefine our world in ways we can scarcely imagine. Only by adhering to the principles of divine order and moral integrity can we hope to counter the rising tide of global control and preserve the sanctity of human dignity as ordained by our Creator.

FIVE

A GLOBAL THEOSOPHY

CULTURAL MARIONETTISTS

Major historical influences, like occult feminism, shamanism, and hermetic practices, as discussed in earlier chapters, have undeniably laid the groundwork for the resurgence of Paganism in today's culture, but cultural movements are seldom driven by ideology alone. Behind every transformative shift lies a complex web of shadowy figures and organizations, providing the resources and strategies necessary to deceive the masses. Unlike Christianity, which, though supported by faith-based nonprofits and influential believers, is primarily fueled by personal transformation and testimony, the agendas of Marxist ideologies and modern Paganism rely heavily on the orchestration of powerful marionettists—those who pull the strings behind the scenes. These figures and organizations skillfully leverage financial resources, global networks, and strategic influence to shape public perception and steer cultural shifts, all while remaining largely unseen.

While Christianity spreads organically through the genuine faith experiences of individuals, the resurgence of Paganism is anything but spontaneous. It is meticulously crafted and imposed from above, with every move calculated to reshape society in alignment with its hidden objectives. The populace, often unaware of the forces at play, gradually adopts a worldview that has been deliberately engineered by these unseen puppeteers.

This resurgence is not merely a grassroots movement of individuals reclaiming ancient practices; it is chiefly driven by elite ideologues who adhere to radical theosophic and hermetic philosophies. These influential figures, often operating in the shadows, seek to inject their Pagan aspirations into society to reshape the world according to their esoteric beliefs. However, their true agenda is masked by the more visible and sensational forms of Paganism—such as the rise of witchcraft and Wicca among the general populace—which serve as convenient distractions. This sleight of hand allows the true architects of the movement to operate with minimal scrutiny.

This tactic is akin to the "motte and bailey" strategy mentioned in a previous chapter. The "motte" represents the radical and indefensible aspects of modern Paganism, such as extreme public displays or controversial practices, which naturally draw the attention and criticism of the public. Meanwhile, the "bailey" comprises the more guarded, esoteric, and socially palatable beliefs of these elites, shielded from direct criticism by the public's focus on the visible extremes. As a result, while opposition often targets the overt expressions—like trans parades, abortion advocacy, and other prominent causes—the deeper, more underhanded currents of thought, where the true power and influence reside, continue to steer the cultural tide largely unchallenged.

In the following section, the focus shifts to the key players orchestrating this movement—the individuals and groups who are not only shaping contemporary thought but also directing societal change from behind the scenes. By examining the roles and agendas of these central figures and unmasking those who are truly pulling the strings, it becomes evident how deeply intertwined financial power, ideological zeal, and a technocratic lust for dominance are in the current resurgence of Paganism. Understanding who is orchestrating these efforts is crucial to grasping the broader implications of this cultural shift.

EVOLUTIONARY LEADERS

"There is a cult behind our radical culture shift and their name is the Evolutionary Leaders,"[1] warns Lisa Logan, a parental rights advocate and leading expert on the hidden dangers of Social Emotional Learning programs. The group in question, Evolutionary Leaders, consists of prominent members including futurists, artists, PhDs, philanthropists, and spiritual leaders such as Deepak Chopra, Bruce Lipton, and the late Barbara Marx Hubbard. Describing themselves as "a community of thought leaders from diverse disciplines who come together in synergy to help support a shift in consciousness,"[2] the Evolutionary Leaders, according to Logan, are secretly promoting "Gnostic ideas into society" based upon "a world religion called New Thought."

Shining a light on the group's true intentions, Logan posted on X:

> As the name suggests, this cult's beliefs have a lot to
> do with evolution. Specifically, that global cooperation
> (communism) is how the next big evolutionary leap into
> an evolved species being with greater awareness is going to
> happen. Individualism/free will is not an option. . . . This
> is not just some fringe cult with no power or influence. The
> Evolutionary Leaders are tied into the big business initiatives
> of ESG, are putting their religion into schools via Social
> Emotional Learning and are working with the UN to install
> a global one world religion.[3]

Logan's concerns expose a deeper issue with the Evolutionary Leaders' agenda: A cultic and Pagan worldview embedded within their vision for global transformation. Blending ancient occult practices with contemporary ideological frameworks, the Evolutionary Leaders, and their allies at the United Nations, seek to create a "global community"[4] with a "unitary consciousness."[5] This worldview not only challenges traditional religious beliefs but also seeks to reconfigure societal structures in alignment with their Marxist-inspired Gnostic reimagining of planet Earth.

To illustrate this transformative cultic worldview, consider the warped perspective of Barbara Marx Hubbard, a prominent figure among the Evolutionary Leaders. In her book *Conscious Evolution*, Hubbard articulates a vision of humanity's evolution that intertwines spiritual and scientific aspirations, reflecting the very essence of their ominous agenda:

In traditional religious language, we were created in the image of God and are becoming ever more godlike. In evolutionary language, we were created by the process of evolution and are becoming coevolutionary with that process. In cocreation we weave together two strands—our spiritual essence and our scientific and social capacities—to participate in the creation. When these strands blend, a new human is born: a universal human, one awakened through the heart to the whole of life, moved from within to express life purpose in the world, opening up to a cosmic consciousness. We become cocreators, unique and personal expressions of the divine, precisely because our creativity is so activated. The most fundamental step on the path of the cocreator is a new spirituality in which we shift our relationship with the creative process from creature to cocreator—from unconscious to conscious evolution.

According to Hubbard, the goal of conscious evolution, a central belief of the Evolutionary Leaders, is to create a "universal human" that acts as a "cocreator" of a "new spirituality." For Hubbard, the birth of the universal human isn't a solitary path, but one that humanity must all embark on together as a collective. Thus, the universal human is representative of a new global human brain—a communist oneness in which all people become gods, or what she calls "cocreators," capable of inspiring a new planetary evolution toward a greater so-called divine expression.

To realize this grand vision, Hubbard and her fellow Evolutionary Leaders employ one of the most powerful Marxist strategies: seizing control over the means of production. In this context, the "means of production" is not just economic but psychological. By embedding their agenda into major global initiatives like ESG (Environmental, Social, and Governance) and infiltrating educational systems through Social Emotional Learning and sex education, these leaders aim to shape and control the collective human mind. This approach serves as a redesigned Tower of Babel, where the true power lies in controlling thought and ideology at a global scale.

The Evolutionary Leaders' plan requires universal participation, pushing for a new form of collectivism that transforms individual minds into components of a greater, shared consciousness. This technocratic ambition not only seeks to influence global institutions but also aims to reshape societal values and beliefs, making their cultic and Pagan ideologies pervasive and pernicious.

ROBERT MULLER: THE ARCHITECT
BEHIND THE CURTAIN

To fully grasp the spiritual and social forces driving the Evolutionary Leaders, it is essential to pull back the curtain on the figures and ideologies that have shaped their worldview. While the Evolutionary Leaders are a relatively recent phenomenon, their agenda is deeply rooted in the ideas and movements that preceded them. One such looming figure is Robert Muller, a former Assistant Secretary-General of the United Nations, whose radical beliefs and ambitious plans offer crucial insights into the current resurgence of Paganism and its intersection with global governance.

Muller, often hailed as the "father of global education,"[6] played a pivotal role in shaping the United Nations' spiritual, educational, and developmental frameworks. His vision for a transformed global society was marked by a blend of utopian idealism and technocratic ambition. Muller's radical views on global governance and his call for the United Nations to serve as "the global brain of humanity" in a new world order reveal the deep-seated Pagan and Marxist influences behind the Evolutionary Leaders' agenda.

Muller's ideas were not merely abstract notions; they were designed to reshape global institutions and societal norms. In his writings, Muller espoused a vision for humanity that entailed a profound overhaul of traditional values and structures. He proposed that humanity's progress depended on eradicating perceived evils such as materialism, nationalism, and overconsumption—concepts he saw as barriers to achieving a higher state of collective consciousness.

Consider this alarming excerpt from Muller's work:

The human species represents an extraordinary progress of evolution on this planet. It will be even more astonishing, provided we weed out the mistakes and wrong objectives which went to our heads: enrichment, armaments, national sovereignty, militarization, overconsumption, waste on colossal scales, destruction of other species and of nature, violence, materialism, racial and sexual discrimination, overpopulation, extreme wealth side by side with extreme poverty, etc. These evils and wrong courses have been well identified by the United Nations, the planet-wide, human-wide evolutionary meta-organism.

Muller's vision extended beyond mere criticism; he advocated for a radical transformation of global institutions under the direction of the United Nations, which would serve as a central arbiter of truth and morality. He suggested renaming and reforming the United Nations into the "Earth Organization" and eventually into the "Metaglobal Cosmic Organization," where science, religion, and indigenous wisdom would converge to dictate human behavior and institutional frameworks. At its core, Muller's message is at odds with Christian teachings. His "2,000 Ideas for a New World Order," which was later expanded to over 7,000 ideas, advocates for a restructured global society that dismisses traditional Christian values in favor of a new worldview driven by technocratic control and esoteric spirituality. Such an agenda undermines foundational Christian principles of individual sovereignty and divine providence. Instead of a faith-based, individual relationship with God, Muller's proposals advocate for a collectivist, human-centered system that seeks to impose a universal order contrary to the scriptural understanding of divine authority and moral order.

For example, Muller proposed:

- The creation of a "Permanent Religious Parliament" or "Spiritual Agency of the United Nations," superseding existing religious authorities or denominational bodies.
- That national sovereignty be replaced by "Earth sovereignty," in which the United Nations would act as the central governing power.
- The creation of a "World Year of Forgiveness" in which all people seek "the Earth, nature, the air, the oceans and our brethren animals" for forgiveness for the pain and suffering we as humans have caused them.
- A significant reduction in masculinity and an increase in femininity the world over.
- That the United Nations' "peace-keeping services" be the only military on Earth allowed to use the phrase "God with us."
- The formation of a "UN World Income Information Bureau" that would track the individual income of everyone on the planet to ensure that equity is maintained.
- The creation of a "World Compliance Council" overseen by the United Nations.
- That the curriculum of the United Nations "should be taught in every school on Earth."
- Through his "prophecy" that the United Nations would become "the mind, the heart, and the soul of humanity" and the "epicenter of all human thinking and efforts."
- An evolution of humanity in which we "go beyond globalism" by transforming "the UN into the first Metaglobal Cosmic Organization of the Earth and nature-conscious human species."

- That "Mother Earth" should be renamed "Goddess Earth" in honor of Gaia.[7]
- That God's only mistake in creation was making man.[8]

Muller's radical agenda wasn't an isolated phenomenon; it was part of a broader, more brazen movement to reshape global governance. His vision for a new world order, laced with technocratic control and Pagan spirituality, echoes the ambitions of others who have held significant influence within the United Nations. One prominent figure in this scheme was Julian Huxley, a historical inspiration to the Evolutionary Leaders who served as the first Director-General of UNESCO. Huxley, a British biologist and evolutionary humanist himself, who "used his position at UNESCO to propagandize the subject of 'birth control.'"[9]

He was instrumental in laying the ideological foundations for a new global order. His contributions provided a template for the radical, globalist ideas that Muller later championed. Together with Muller and other technocratic Pagans, Huxley helped forge a framework for global governance that continues to this day.

THE SOCIALIST STATE

In a pluralistic society, religious freedoms are a cornerstone of our values, allowing for a diversity of beliefs, even when they differ from a Christian worldview. This is inherent to our religious liberties, where people are free to practice their faith without interference. However, the problem arises when a Pagan religious system, such as New Thought or Theosophy, masquerades as a philosophy or social initiative, craftily coercing a broader agenda. These frameworks are insidiously steering us toward a socialist technocratic state seeking to impose a uniform worldview, guided by elites at the United Nations, under the guise of social progress and modernity.

This threat was forewarned to Americans by W. Cleon Skousen in his 1958 work, *The Naked Communist*, where he explains that a key Marxist objective is to "promote the UN as the only hope for mankind" and "demand that it be set up as one-world government with its own independent armed forces."[10]

Unpacking the real agenda of the United Nations, Skousen writes:

> *The UN is described as a "second try" for a new world order. However, its multitude of treaties, programs and agendas that promote socialism and the dismantling of traditional Western values has discredited it as a unifying organization. It does not have freedom's best interests in mind but seeks to centralize world power into a single body. In 2009, a call for "global democracy" was introduced at the UN. The following year, a UN body urged support for a treaty that would regulate private military and security companies. Hundreds of other UN proclamations called for socialist/communist agenda items including national health care, acquiescence by all nations to a world court, subservience to the world's collective will, and the institutionalization of a new moral structure superseding the people's will. Proponents of the UN see this collective power as the great equalizer. But, at the center of this utopian dream is the necessity of weakening the United States as a world power. As the U.S. loses its prominence as the standard-bearer of liberty, so tyranny has risen in other parts of the world.*[11]

Essentially, what individuals like Logan and Skousen are warning about is the rise of an unofficial state-sponsored Pagan religion. Undermining traditional Christian values to reshape society in their image, figures like Robert Muller, Julian Huxley, and the Evolutionary Leaders, alongside the UN, exemplify how godless Pagan religions and corrupt political ambitions are being merged into a cohesive tyrannical ideology. But as Skousen details, for this "utopian dream" to be successful, the United States must first be weakened. According to Dr. Jim Richards, the only way for antichrist technocratic individuals and institutions to deteriorate the strength of this country and overthrow the existing societal order must involve the introduction of a period of "demoralization."[12]

Richard depicts this process as:

Demoralization is not simply the attempt to lead people into immoral living; it is the attempt to lead people to lawlessness (iniquity). Destroy the consciousness of God. Let man determine good and evil for himself and he will oppress himself.

Adding to his definition, Richard explains that as the consciousness of God is destroyed in a society, systems inevitably collapse, and chaos ensues. For the Marxist, this is all an intentional step to create demoralization. Mass inflation, economic collapse, riots, illegal immigration, and spikes in the crime rate are all tangible forms of demoralization that, once initiated, serve to level the old societal structures, so that a new Marxist and godless system can be erected. "Once we are demoralized," Richards reminds us, "the state is our source of hope and protection."[13]

The socialist principle of demoralization, or the purposeful creation of chaos within a society to act as a reboot on the existing structures and values, helps us make more sense of former Vice President Kamala Harris' often-repeated phrase, "What can be, unburdened by what has been."[14] More than word salad or the deranged ramblings of an inebriated woman of a certain age, Harris' favorite saying is a socialist tell pointing to her spiritual and political ambitions to "unburden" America from its foundational frameworks of personal liberty and the Christian faith.

In a recent interview with conservative thought leader and President of Turning Point USA, Charlie Kirk, Dr. James Lindsay called Harris' catchphrase "a Marxist incantation" reminiscent of China's Mao Zedong's Red Guard's infamous phrase "Smash the Old World, Build the New World" or attempts by Bolshevik revolutionaries to radically transform Russian society and create a "new man" through the imposition of communist ideals.[15]

This is why the notion of a Harris presidency was so frightening! Together with former President Biden, Harris has already "unburdened" the United States from many of its foundational principles. The demoralizing duo, who ushered in "the worst cost-of-living crisis in 20 years,"[16] also created a world of massive inflation, allowed record illegal immigration, failed to protect American youth from deadly fentanyl, and stood idly by as an army of scantily clad drag queens paraded themselves in front of our nation's schoolchildren.

But is this demoralization a cause or merely a symptom? In a way, it's both. Yes, these actions—or lack thereof—by Biden and Harris have undeniably contributed to the erosion of America's moral fabric. Yet, it's also true that their policies have taken root in a society already demoralized, a society conditioned by the corrosive influence of digital platforms and social media with an obvious bent toward bankrupting our nation's ethical compass. Through platforms like Instagram, TikTok, and Snapchat, Americans are bombarded with distorted videos, live feeds, and posts that desensitize them to Pagan ideologies, such as witchcraft and tarot readings, sexually distorted content featuring nudity and LGBTQ+ ideology, and a violent subculture showcasing pro-Hamas rhetoric, antisemitic extremism, and hate speech toward Christians. As we will see, this toxic digital environment fosters a culture where moral relativism reigns, paving the way for policies that further entrench a Pagan decay.

TECHNOPAGANISM

"Without the sacred, there is no differentiation in space. If we are about to enter cyberspace, the first thing we must do is plant the divine in it,"[17] confessed Mark Pesce in an interview with *Wired* magazine. Pesce, an openly gay futurist[18] and self-professed "technopagan," represents "a startling number"[19] of individuals who have merged Pagan spirituality with modern technology. Unlike computer engineers and their other secular counterparts, technopagans see digital spaces as realms where they can manipulate and even play God—using algorithms, data, and virtual reality as tools for spiritual creation and ideological control.

As Erik Davis wrote in *Wired*,

> *Magic is the science of the imagination, the art of engineering consciousness and discovering the virtual forces that connect the body-mind with the physical world. And technopagans suspect that these occult Old Ways can provide some handy tools and tactics in our dizzying digital environment of intelligent agents.*[20]

For Pesce, who has played a key role in shaping and predicting virtual reality, the digital realm is more than just a technological tool—it's divine. Drawing from the ancient teachings of Hermes Trismegistus, Pesce believes that hermetic principles can be applied to data and technology, integrating them into the "circle of human life" that he sees as inherently divine. Pesce, who blends Pagan rituals with cyberspace, such as gathering a "crew of mostly gay men into a circle"[21] to perform a "digitally enhanced"[22] ritual celebration of the dead around Halloween, claims, "I think computers can be as sacred as we are because they can embody our communication with each other and with the entities—the divine parts of ourselves—that we invoke in that space."[23]

Invoking the hermetic imagery of a snake eating its own tail, otherwise known as Ouroboros, which itself is a Pagan picture of "as above, so below," Pesce claims a spiritual rebirth regarding the World Wide Web, in which he saw "the Web eating the Net." For the non-technical reader, this analogy might require more explanation, but the important takeaway isn't what Pesce meant, but rather the explicit evidence the analogy offers that technopagans' digital experiences are being shaped by hermetic and Pagan ideology.

From a Christian worldview, Pesce's technopaganism is not a sign of progress but of spiritual peril. It's a continuation of mankind's age-old attempt to dethrone God and replace divine order with human constructs. The digital age has simply provided a new landscape—a virtual frontier—for this rebellion to unfold. What we're seeing is not merely a fascination with technology but a deeper ideological shift: a pursuit of utopia within cyberspace, where technopagans believe they can remake reality itself according to their desires.

- *Augmented Reality.* Through augmented reality (AR), technopagans are reshaping how children and teens engage with the world, blending fantasy and reality. By immersing users in digital environments that glorify Pagan rituals or anti-Christian symbols, they subtly influence impressionable minds to embrace a spiritual reality that distances them from biblical truth.

- *Digital Avatars.* Virtual avatars, especially popular in gaming and social media, are being used to promote Pagan ideologies. Teens and young adults are encouraged to create digital versions of themselves that explore unbiblical identities or spiritual powers, altering their sense of self and opening the door to moral confusion and identity crises, all while disconnecting from the God-given value of their physical existence.
- *Cyberspace.* For technopagans, cyberspace represents a new spiritual frontier where they manipulate reality to promote their worldview. Children, who spend much of their time online, are being exposed to this growing ideology where ancient Pagan beliefs about gods, mysticism, and altered realities are normalized in the digital realm, shaping their spiritual understanding and diverting them away from Christianity.
- *Programming Reality.* Technopagans believe they can "program" reality by using data and algorithms to influence outcomes in the physical world. This pursuit of control has infiltrated the tech industry, where social media platforms shape young minds, driving teens toward a worldview rooted in moral relativism and self-worship. This manipulation not only erodes their moral foundation but also impacts relationships and causes confusion about truth, love, and responsibility.
- *Digital Art.* The rise of digital art, including NFTs and virtual installations, has become another avenue for Pagan ideologies. By embedding spiritual or occult symbols in the art that children and teens consume online, technopagans use visual media to subtly reshape perceptions of spirituality, encouraging the worship of nature, self, or false gods while pushing Christian values

further to the margins. These influences permeate online spaces, from environmentalism linked to Earth worship to the promotion of unbiblical moral frameworks in relationships.

While none of these technologies is inherently evil in and of themselves, Christians must use discernment, as often those behind these new technologies are driven by Pagan ideological pursuits and a Marxist vision of utopia. Historically, Marxists sought to build an ideal society here on Earth, reshaping social, political, and economic systems through revolution. Today's technopagans have shifted that battleground to digital spaces, believing that virtual worlds can become the new canvases upon which to paint their ideals. Both movements share the same fundamental desire—to recreate Eden without God. But this vision of a virtual utopia is inherently flawed.

It is within this context that we must understand the broader cultural demoralization at play. Just as Marxist ideals seek to undermine traditional values and discredit moral foundations in society, technopaganism seeks to do the same through the medium of technology. What we are witnessing is not a new movement, but the latest iteration of an ancient rebellion against God, dressed in the garb of digital innovation.

In many ways, these technological Pagans see themselves as the architects of a new world order—one built not on the laws of nature or divine order, but on the principles of self-deification and virtual control. Like the "man of lawlessness"[24] described in Scripture, they exalt themselves above everything that is called God, attempting to establish their dominion over this Earth as if they were gods. The irony is that their pursuit of utopia will only lead to further moral decay, confusion, and disconnection from the true source of life and purpose: the Creator God.

DEMORALIZATION

What we are witnessing on these digital battlegrounds is the harvest of seeds planted long ago. The demoralization of society didn't begin overnight; it had been cultivated for years, long before Harris stepped into office. More than a half-century ago, Skousen pointed out that communists planned to "belittle all forms of American culture,"[25] "discredit the American founding fathers,"[26] "discredit the American Constitution,"[27] and "break down cultural standards of morality."[28] Today, that very playbook is being followed, as figures like Harris, Biden, President Barack Obama, and President Bill Clinton and his wife Hillary, work to embed a spirit of demoralization deep within the American psyche. Thus, it was no surprise when President Trump, during the second presidential debate in the summer of 2024,[29] blasted Harris with the statement, "She's a Marxist—everybody knows she's a Marxist! Her father is a Marxist professor in economics, and he taught her well."[30]

Trump's comment underscores a broader, critical point: Harris represents just one individual within a larger ideological movement characterized by Marxist succession. This ideological lineage involves a concerted effort to instill and perpetuate Marxist values across generations, each passing down a legacy of radicalism that has now become ingrained in various levels of American leadership and society.

This transformation has been carefully engineered with digital platforms playing a pivotal role in redefining societal norms. By constantly feeding users content that blurs the lines between acceptable and taboo, these platforms have conditioned society to accept, and even embrace, what was once considered immoral or fringe. The algorithms don't just reflect the culture—they actively shape it, creating a digital ecosystem where the erosion of traditional values is not just allowed but encouraged.

In this new age, social media platforms have evolved far beyond mere communication tools; they've transformed into modern-day digital-walled Pagan temples. Here, posts are offered as sacrifices, and views become a form of communal ritual gathering. Just as ancient devotees once performed Pagan rites to appease their gods, today's digital denizens engage in a different kind of ritual: content creation and consumption. Women, for instance, may present their bodies for views or even turn to platforms like OnlyFans, commodifying themselves in a manner reminiscent of ancient temple prostitutes.

Algorithms on platforms like TikTok have relentlessly fed Americans a steady diet of distorted videos and posts, shaping public perception and normalizing what was once considered taboo. For example, the rapid mainstreaming of gender confusion has been largely fueled by TikTok's algorithm, which aggressively promotes transgender influencers and "transition journeys" to young users. What was once a rare psychological condition is now a celebrated identity, with social media rewarding those who publicly embrace it.[31]

The question then becomes: Which came first? Is the demoralization driven by political leadership, or is the demoralization perpetuated and accelerated by social media? In truth, they are part of the same cycle—one feeding off the other, each intensifying the other's impact on society. As this cycle continues, it pushes us further down a path where Pagan ideologies and moral relativism gain ground, all under the watchful eye of a technocratic elite.

THE HIVE BRAIN:
A TECHNOCRATIC NIGHTMARE

One such individual, Klaus Schwab, the architect behind the World Economic Forum and chief proponent of The Great Reset, isn't just pushing for technological advancement—he's advocating for something far more dangerous. Under the veneer of progress, Schwab and his technocratic allies are seeking to rewire humanity's very essence through what they call a "hive brain." This isn't just about creating smarter technology or improving connectivity—it's about reshaping human consciousness itself, paving the way for a form of collective control that smacks of a totalitarian dystopia.

In Schwab's own words, the future requires "immediate, persistent, and decisive collective action"[32] from all sectors of society. But what he truly means is that this "collective action" will be impossible unless we adopt collective thinking. During a conversation at the World Economic Forum, he made his ambitions clear: "Can you imagine that in 10 years when we are sitting here, we have an implant in all of our brains, and I can immediately feel . . . how some people will react to your answers."[33] For Schwab, the path to this collective action isn't just through policy—it's through rewiring the very minds of the global population.

Enter the hive brain, a concept that envisions individuals submitting their autonomy to a global network of artificial intelligence and technological systems that act as a single, unified intelligence. This is not an abstract idea. Schwab is pushing for a world where independent thought and personal freedoms are sacrificed on the altar of efficiency and global governance.

The notion of a hive brain isn't just futuristic—it's frighteningly Pagan. Throughout history, Pagan systems sought to obliterate individual identity, merging the self into a greater cosmic order. Whether through mystical rites or occult practices, the end goal was always the same: the erasure of individuality in favor of a collective oneness. Schwab's vision is no different, though it's dressed up in the language of technological progress. He's repackaging the same Pagan desire for collective control, but this time using AI and digital infrastructure to strip people of their God-given autonomy.

This Great Reset, underpinned by the idea of collective intelligence, seeks to unify human thought into a global consciousness that operates more like a machine than a society. Individual thought? Outdated. Personal freedom? A relic of the past. What Schwab and his ilk desire is a world where human beings are reduced to mere data points in a vast network, with decisions dictated not by personal conscience or moral standards, but by algorithms designed to promote compliance and control.

This isn't just dangerous—it's deeply anti-human. The Christian worldview teaches that each person is made in the image of God, with unique value, purpose, and autonomy. Schwab's hive brain model, by contrast, strips away that individuality, treating humans as little more than nodes in a grand technological scheme. And while Schwab might argue that this is necessary for a better, more efficient future, the reality is that it's a blatant power grab—a way to concentrate control into the hands of a few elite technocrats who would set themselves up as the rulers of this new digital empire.

Louis Rosenberg, an influential figure in augmented reality and artificial intelligence, explains that collective intelligence works by creating "a brain of brains"[34] through human vibration. (Remember the Hermetic principle of vibration we discussed earlier?) Lisa Logan warns that this "hive brain" is "a coordinated effort to take . . . cognitive liberty from all of us." She adds that:

Your spiritual beliefs are being hacked, whether you know it or not, by a literal neo-communist religious cult. This cult is the cause of all the Woke ideas you see suddenly permeating our culture. They believe that the only way to save the human race from extinction and make the next evolutionary leap to transform society into a new higher species of human is to join together in global cooperation and community into a collective superorganism.

Efforts by groups like the World Economic Forum and the Evolutionary Leaders to organize society into a single "collective superorganism" feel frighteningly reminiscent of control exhibited by the beast in Revelations 13, in which it possesses "authority over every tribe, people, language, and nation" by making them "receive a mark" on their right hand or forehead.

While it may be too early to decisively say if we are in the end times, the signs of deception are all around us. Many Christians are already acquiescing and unknowingly adopting Pagan beliefs into their faith. As believers, the goal must be to remain steadfast and vigilant, guarding against deception. As Jesus warned in Matthew 24:24, "For false messiahs and false prophets will arise and perform great signs and wonders to lead astray, if possible, even the elect." The push for a hive brain—whether it comes in the form of technological control, collective intelligence, or any other effort to unify thought under a secular, Pagan system—represents exactly the kind of deception Jesus spoke of. Those who follow Christ must not be fooled by the promises of efficiency or global cooperation at the expense of their God-given identity and autonomy. Instead, we must keep our eyes fixed on the Creator and resist the allure of becoming gods ourselves. For it is in that temptation that true destruction lies, and, as we will see, unfortunately, some who call themselves Christians have already taken a bite of its fruit.

SIX

PAGAN CHRISTIANITY

Error, indeed, is never set forth in its naked deformity,
lest, being thus exposed, it should at once be detected.
But it is craftily decked out in an attractive dress,
so as, by its outward form, to make it appear to the
inexperienced more true than the truth itself.

—Irenaeus, *Against Heresies, Book 1*, Preface

Throughout history, the church has been forced to recalibrate itself time after time as it bounces back from the extremes of countless false ideologies. The pendulum of truth often swings between the poles of legalism on one side and licentiousness on the other. This was clearly exhibited in the first two heresies to challenge the early church—the Judaizers, who clung to legalistic adherence to the Law of Moses, and the Gnostics, who veered into superstitious spiritual elitism and a disregard for the body. As Irenaeus warned in the early centuries, error is rarely presented in its raw form; instead, it is "craftily decked out in an attractive dress," appearing to offer more truth and insight than genuine doctrine to the spiritually naive. This pattern continues to play out in our modern world, as many of today's Christians fall for the decorative deception of a new form of Gnosticism: Pagan Christianity.

Like all heresies, Pagan Christianity is a hybrid of orthodox Christian teachings combined with the seductive falsehoods of Pagan ideology. It borrows from the language of the faith,

117

cloaking itself in the familiar while quietly distorting the Gospel's core. This blending of truth and error introduces not just a gray area, but actual heresy—where elements of Paganism and worldly philosophies are mistakenly embraced. While some believers may unknowingly hold to aspects of these false teachings without negating their faith, others have fully embraced these errors leading them into apostasy. This often manifests as a form of deconstructionism, where foundational Christian beliefs are gradually dismantled and replaced with soft forms of witchcraft, mysticism, Gnosticism ideology, and at times, the ultimate spiritual rebellion—Atheism.

Typically, these beliefs first leach into the faith's groundwater through emerging social trends. Perhaps the best example of this in recent years was the explosive reception within Christian circles of the Enneagram, advertised as a complex personality test purported to assist users in self-discovery. But in fact, it is a cultic tool developed by accessing "spirit guides."

THE ENNEAGRAM AND THE OCCULT

"It came from my own observations, but mostly from automatic writing,"[1] stated Claudio Naranjo, a spiritualist and psychiatrist credited with developing the Enneagram diagram into a personality test, when asked how he expanded the system. Naranjo openly admitted that his version of the Enneagram wasn't merely the result of scientific or psychological inquiry but was also deeply influenced by automatic writing, a controversial practice rooted in spiritualism. This method, often regarded as a form of divination or channeling, involves allowing one's hand to write words without conscious control, supposedly guided by a spiritual force or the subconscious.

From a Christian viewpoint, this revelation about the Enneagram's development is alarming. Automatic writing is considered a form of occultism, forbidden in Scripture due to its association with opening oneself up to spiritual influences outside of God's authority. For instance, in Deuteronomy 18:10-12, we are instructed:

> No one among you is to sacrifice his son or daughter in
> the fire, practice divination, tell fortunes, interpret omens,
> practice sorcery, cast spells, consult a medium or a spiritist,
> or inquire of the dead. Everyone who does these acts is
> detestable to the Lord, and the Lord your God is driving out
> the nations before you because of these detestable acts.[2]

Clearly, a practice like automatic writing or contacting a "higher source"[3] other than God for revelation, would be condemned alongside the other practices mentioned in this passage as a form of communicating with spirits. Naranjo's admission reveals that the Enneagram, now popularized in many Christian circles, has spiritual origins that conflict with biblical teachings. In fact, Naranjo, as well as his mentor Oscar Ichazo, borrowed the diagram of the Enneagram from Georges Gurdjieff, a spiritual esoteric and occultist who believed that the Enneagram contained within it the secrets of the universe.

According to Gurdjieff's biographer Stephen A. Grant, Gurdjieff "especially admired Mme. Blavatsky"[4] and harmonized his use of the esoteric with hers.[5] According to Grant, Gurdjieff first read Blavatsky when he was 21, at which time "he took her indications seriously."[6] Grant writes:

> Gurdjieff was an insatiable reader of books on supernatural
> phenomena and ancient spiritual traditions. At the time,

the most celebrated work among occult seekers in Europe
was Isis Unveiled, authored by the redoubtable Helena
Petrovna Blavatsky, who asserted that Christianity and
other traditional religions were based on a common esoteric
doctrine that had originated thousands of years earlier in
India and spread over centuries through Assyria, Egypt,
and Greece.

After reading the works of Blavatsky, Gurdjieff "combined a mystical understanding of Christianity with a deep commitment to Buddhism and Buddhist practice,"[7] despite eventually distancing himself from her due to "controversy within the Theosophy movement."[8] His teachings, along with those of his contemporaries, gave rise to what he termed "esoteric Christianity," a fusion of the teachings of Jesus combined with a "synthesis of Western science and Eastern spirituality."[9]

Despite the obvious Pagan roots of the Enneagram, as exemplified in the lives and teachings of Gurdjieff, Ichazo, and Naranjo, many Christians blindly (while others knowingly) use it as a tool for leadership training, relationship compatibility, and even guiding parenting styles. Eclipsing the role of the Holy Spirit for some, believers are relying on Enneagram scores for personal and spiritual guidance like some sort of Christian horoscope.

This growing trend highlights the subtle infiltration of non-biblical Pagan practices into Christian circles, often without discerning the deeper spiritual implications of recognizing such practices' roots in esoteric and Pagan traditions. Part of the deception is making these practices appear doctrinally sound. As with the Enneagram, its rise in cultural popularity led to books like *The Enneagram: A Christian Perspective*, *Bible Promises for the Enneagram*, and *The Enneagram for Beginners: A Christian Guide* to *Understanding Your Type for a God-Oriented Life*, all designed to appeal to a Christian audience.

As concerning as the use of the Enneagram is, it's only one of many ways that Christians are currently embracing Pagan practices. From transcendental meditation to crystals and astrology, there are numerous trends creeping into the church, often under the guise of self-improvement or spiritual wellness. These practices, like the Enneagram, may seem harmless on the surface but they carry deeper spiritual implications that conflict with biblical Christianity. To discern these influences, believers must understand their origins, assess their compatibility with Scripture, and develop a biblical worldview on how to address them.

Belial and Christ

Well acquainted with spiritual warfare and demonic powers, the Apostle Paul understood the dangers of mixing Pagan practices with Christian beliefs. In his second letter to the Corinthian church, he warns:

> Don't become partners with those who do not believe.
> For what partnership is there between righteousness and
> lawlessness? Or what fellowship does light have with darkness?
> What agreement does Christ have with Belial? Or what does a
> believer have in common with an unbeliever?[10]

Paul's language here is deliberate. According to *Vine's Expository Dictionary of New Testament Words*, the term "Belial" was originally used to signify "extreme wickedness"[11] and eventually became an "epithet of Satan."[12] For Paul, this was not a mere metaphor but a serious reminder that believers have no business blending the faith with practices rooted in Paganism or demonic influence. He saw such compromises as dangerously incompatible with the purity and holiness that should characterize the life of a believer.

Yet today, despite Paul's clear warning, many Christians are embracing practices with roots in Pagan spirituality, often rationalizing these choices as harmless or spiritually enlightening. By discounting the Word of God, they risk opening themselves to influences that are not only unbiblical but directly opposed to the kingdom of light. Believers must remember that pursuing spiritual wellness or self-improvement cannot come at the cost of compromising biblical truth. A clear stance is essential: True freedom and spiritual power come through Christ alone, not through practices tainted by darkness.

To examine these issues more closely, it's important to identify specific practices that have gained popularity within Christian circles, often under the guise of spirituality or personal growth. By breaking down each practice, we can better understand its origins and implications, and the subtle ways it conflicts with biblical teaching. This exploration will help clarify how these trends, though enticing, lead believers away from a Christ-centered faith and introduce elements that align more with Pagan or occult philosophies than with Scripture.

Let's now look at these practices individually and consider the spiritual dangers they pose and the biblical response.

Pagan Practice: Crystals
Description of the Practice: Crystals are often used for their supposed healing properties or as a means of spiritual alignment. Types of crystals are used to channel energy or frequency for specific needs, such as healing, wealth, and love.

Christian Response: Crystals present multiple problems for the believer. They ascribe healing power to forces outside of God, thus becoming idols. They direct man to trust in physical matter, rather than Christ for their healing. And they ascribe positive supernatural energy apart from God.

Pagan Practice: Burning Sage and House Cleansing Rituals

Description of the Practice: Rooted in indigenous and Pagan spiritual practices, burning sage is believed to cleanse spaces of negative energy and evil spirits, invite peace, and purify individuals. Often detached from its cultural significance, the practice is frequently associated with New Age spirituality, witchcraft, and occult practices.

Christian Response: Burning sage for spiritual purposes may seem like a harmless or even meaningful practice, but it conflicts with the Bible's teaching on spiritual warfare and cleansing. As Paul reminds us, "The weapons of our warfare are not of the flesh but have divine power to destroy strongholds" (2 Corinthians 10:4). The Bible is clear that it is the blood of Christ—His sacrifice on the cross—that cleanses us from sin and overcomes evil (Hebrews 9:14, 1 John 1:7). Smoke, herbs, or any physical ritual cannot replace the redemptive and purifying power of Christ. Relying on such practices risks placing trust in material things rather than in the sufficiency of Christ's work.

Pagan Practice: Yoga and Transcendental Meditation
Description of the Practice: Yoga, rooted in Hinduism, combines physical postures, breathing techniques, and meditation to align the body, mind, and spirit with spiritual energies. While often marketed as exercise, its spiritual origins remain central to its practice. Transcendental meditation, derived from Hindu traditions, involves silently repeating a mantra to achieve relaxation and heightened awareness, aiming to connect with a universal or cosmic force. Both practices emphasize inward focus and spiritual awakening.

Christian Response: While stretching and physical exercise are not inherently wrong, Christians should approach practices tied to Pagan worship with caution. The Bible instructs us to meditate on God's Word (Psalm 1:2) and to worship Him alone (Exodus 20:3). Engaging in activities rooted in other religions risks blending faith in Christ with unbiblical elements, potentially shifting focus from the sufficiency of Christ as the sole source of peace and spiritual connection. Whether one can participate in forms of Christian yoga or meditation becomes an issue of personal conscience. This book is not intended to impose rules on exercise practices but encourages believers to prayerfully discern their participation in such activities.

Pagan Practice: Astrology
Description of the Practice: Astrology is the belief that celestial bodies, such as planets and stars, influence human affairs and destinies. This practice, rooted in ancient Paganism and divination, has been used to

predict events, guide decisions, and understand personality traits based on the positions of celestial objects at the time of one's birth. Astrology's origins trace back to Babylonian and Egyptian traditions, and its practices often involve seeking knowledge and control over the future through signs and omens.

Christian Response: Consulting horoscopes or seeking astrological guidance is a form of reliance on created things rather than the Creator (Isaiah 47:13-14). Scripture warns against seeking knowledge through sources other than God, as this opens the door to spiritual deception and idolatry (Deuteronomy 18:9-14). Christians are reminded that their lives are directed by God's will, not the stars (Psalm 139:16, Jeremiah 29:11).

Pagan Practice: Certain Forms of Intercessional Prayer
Description of the Practice: Abuses of intercessional prayer involve practices where individuals use prayer to impose their will onto situations or people, often bypassing the personal agency of others. This can include prayers designed to manipulate someone's choices or circumstances, treating intercession as a form of spiritual coercion. In extreme cases, intercessors might develop elaborate rituals or techniques, believing these actions will compel a desired outcome (pouring salt out, burning candles, or incense). These practices can resemble forms of Christian mysticism or even voodoo-like rituals, where prayer is treated as a tool to control rather than a means of seeking alignment with God's Word and purposes. Such approaches often blur the line between faith-based intercession and superstitious or magical thinking.

Christian Response: As Christians, we are called to "pray without ceasing" (1 Thessalonians 5:17), but our prayers should align with biblical teaching. While intercession is a vital part of the Christian life, radical or unbiblical forms of intercession can devolve into a kind of Christian voodoo, relying on ritualistic methods or formulas rather than the power and authority of Christ. These practices not only risk undermining Christ's role as our ultimate intercessor (Hebrews 7:25), but they can also err by attempting to manipulate someone's free will or personal agency through prayer. Instead, our prayers should honor Christ's unique authority, humbly align with God's will, and respect the dignity and freedom He grants to every individual.

Pagan Practice: Grave Soaking, Veneration of Relics, and Pilgrimage Sites
Description of the Practice: Grave soaking, veneration of relics, and pilgrimage sites are practices rooted in the belief that physical locations or objects hold spiritual significance. Grave soaking involves believers lying on the graves of saints or spiritual leaders, hoping to absorb their spiritual power. The veneration of relics refers to the reverence of physical items, such as the bones or belongings of saints, which are believed to carry divine power. Pilgrimages to holy sites involve traveling to specific locations considered sacred, with the belief that visiting these places can bring spiritual benefits or closer communion with God. These practices often emphasize physical objects or places as conduits for spiritual influence.

Christian Response: In 2 Kings 13:20-21, a man is revived by touching the bones of the prophet Elisha. While this is a remarkable miracle, it is a unique event that showcases God's ability to work miracles, not a standard practice for Christians. This incident does not suggest that physical objects, like bones or graves, hold inherent spiritual power. Rather, it is an example of God's ability to work miracles in His own way. God alone, through His divine will, gives life and healing.

This is important to understand because practices like grave soaking, the veneration of relics, and pilgrimages to sacred sites often imply that physical objects or places can convey spiritual power. However, the Bible teaches that God's power is not transferred through physical means but comes directly from Him. Isaiah 42:8 reminds us that God will not share His glory with anything or anyone else. And in John 14:6, Jesus points to Himself as the only way to the Father. Our focus should remain on seeking God through Christ, not through physical objects or locations. Ultimately, the power of resurrection and healing is from God alone, not relics or human remains.

While visiting historical "holy" sites can stimulate our faith and provide a deeper understanding of our beliefs, it should not be seen as a means of gaining more spiritual power or favor. True spiritual growth comes through our relationship with God, not through physical places or items.

Pagan Practice: Astral Projection
Description of the Practice: Astral projection is a practice in which individuals believe they can separate their spirit or consciousness from their physical body and

travel to different locations, often described as an "out-of-body experience." This practice is rooted in occult and New Age traditions, where practitioners claim they can explore spiritual realms or even interact with other beings. Some see astral projection as a means of spiritual enlightenment or a way to achieve personal transformation, but it is often linked to practices that promote self-reliance and self-discovery apart from God.

Christian Response: Biblically, the practice of astral projection is incompatible with God's design of humanity as spirit, soul, and body (1 Thessalonians 5:23). God created us as whole beings, and our spiritual life is meant to be rooted in our physical bodies, which are temples of the Holy Spirit (1 Corinthians 6:19-20). Astral projection, which seeks to separate the spirit from the body for personal or spiritual gain, contradicts this divine design and can expose individuals to harmful spiritual influences (Deuteronomy 18:10-12).

The Bible does describe "translation" (Acts 8:39-40, 2 Kings 2:11-12), but it is fundamentally different from astral projection. In translation, God moves the whole person, including their physical form, from one place to another. This is a divine act, initiated and controlled by God, and not a practice where the spirit is separated from the body. Unlike astral projection, translation is not about personal exploration or seeking enlightenment but is an extraordinary act of God's sovereign will. Christians are called to seek God through prayer, His Word, and the guidance of the Holy Spirit, not through practices that attempt to separate the spirit from the body.

Pagan Practice: Tarot Card Readings
Description of the Practice: Tarot cards are a form of divination that uses a deck of cards to attempt to gain insight into the future or to receive spiritual guidance. Each card is believed to have specific meanings and symbolism, which practitioners use to interpret a person's fate, behavior, or potential life events. While tarot cards have become widely associated with spiritual and mystical practices, their origins are deeply rooted in occultism and Paganism. Those who use tarot cards often believe that they can tap into unseen forces or energies to guide their lives, making it a form of occult practice that diverts trust away from God's guidance.
Christian Response: The Bible clearly condemns practices like tarot card reading as they involve seeking knowledge from sources other than God. In Deuteronomy 18:10-12, God warns against engaging in divination, fortune-telling, or seeking guidance from occult practices, declaring them to be detestable. While the Holy Spirit can reveal God's will and even aspects of the future to His people (John 16:13, Acts 2:17), the practice of using tarot cards or any other occult means is not a legitimate way to seek divine revelation. Tarot cards attempt to tap into spiritual forces outside of God's will, whereas the Holy Spirit, who indwells believers, provides guidance and wisdom directly from God. As Christians, we are called to rely on the Word of God and the Holy Spirit for direction, understanding, and insight into the future, trusting in God's perfect timing and wisdom (Proverbs 3:5-6).

Pagan Practice: Manifestation Practices

Description of the Practice: Manifestation practices involve the belief that individuals can attract or create their desired outcomes through focused thoughts, feelings, or intentions. This concept is rooted in New Age philosophies, where it is believed that the universe responds to a person's energy or mental focus, bringing about positive events or material gains. Practitioners of manifestation often use visualization, affirmations, and other techniques to align their desires with what they wish to achieve, viewing it as a form of personal empowerment or cosmic law. These practices emphasize the power of the mind in shaping reality, often detached from any spiritual foundation or external authority.

Christian Response: Biblically, faith is not about manifesting any desire or outcome we wish, but about receiving God's promises and precepts as laid out in His Word. True faith involves trusting in God's will and aligning ourselves with His purposes, not trying to manipulate circumstances to fit our personal desires. Scripture teaches that God's plans for us are far greater than we can imagine or desire (Ephesians 3:20), and faith is about surrendering to His good and perfect will. It's through the Holy Spirit that we are empowered to live according to God's Word, not through our own ability to create outcomes through mental focus. Proverbs 3:5-6 reminds us to trust in the Lord with all our hearts, not leaning on our own understanding, and to acknowledge Him in all our ways. True biblical faith is rooted in obedience to God's direction, not in forcing reality to conform to our desires. Charismatic Christians should exercise caution here to ensure that one's faith is directed toward biblical promises, and not personal power or selfish motivations.

Pagan Practice: Energy Healing

Description of the Practice: Energy healing, in its Pagan form, is often rooted in the belief that unseen "life forces" or "energies" within and around the body can be manipulated to heal physical or emotional ailments. This practice can involve techniques like Reiki, chakra balancing, or working with a supposed universal energy that flows through all living things. Practitioners may claim to channel or direct this energy to restore balance or promote healing, relying on their own abilities or spiritual forces that are not rooted in God. These methods often bypass the need for divine intervention, suggesting that healing can occur through human effort or alignment with natural forces.

Christian Response: From a Christian viewpoint, healing is understood to be a divine gift from God, not a force that can be manipulated by human will or spiritual energy. The Bible teaches that healing comes through the power of the Holy Spirit and is often a result of faith in God's will. Healing is not about tapping into an impersonal energy or force but about receiving God's touch through the Holy Spirit's intervention, as seen in Jesus' ministry and the apostles' acts of healing. In charismatic theology, healing is ultimately a supernatural act of God, aligning with His will and purpose. The Holy Spirit empowers believers to minister healing, always directing glory back to God rather than human personalities, power, or energy.

Pagan Practice: Channeling or Seeking Guidance from Spirit Guides

Description of the Practice: Channeling or seeking guidance from spirit guides involves the practice of connecting with, and receiving messages from, supposed spiritual beings or entities that are believed to possess wisdom, knowledge, or power. These spirits are thought to be ancestors, angels, or other supernatural beings that offer insight into a person's life, future, or purpose. Practitioners often use meditation, séances, or other rituals to communicate with these guides, believing that the spirits can provide direction, comfort, or clarity. This practice often emphasizes a personal relationship with these entities and the belief that they can offer guidance outside of traditional religious or scriptural sources.

Christian Response: According to scripture, seeking guidance from spirit guides is seen as incompatible with the biblical understanding of how God communicates with His people. The Bible teaches that believers are to seek guidance and wisdom from the Lord alone (James 1:5), who speaks through His Word and the Holy Spirit. Christians are encouraged to rely on prayer, Scripture, the prompting of the Holy Spirit, and the counsel of Christian fellowship to receive direction, rather than turning to external, spiritual entities. The Bible warns against engaging with spirits other than the Holy Spirit, as these can be deceiving or demonic in nature (1 John 4:1-3).

Pagan Practice: Communicating with the Dead

Description of the Practice: Communicating with the dead involves attempting to contact or communicate with the spirits of deceased individuals. This practice is typically carried out through mediums, séances, or other rituals, with the belief that the dead can provide insight, knowledge, or guidance. People may turn to these practices to seek comfort, answers, or closure from deceased loved ones or to receive messages they believe the dead may offer. It is rooted in spiritualism and often includes practices like reading objects that supposedly carry the spirits' energy or attempting to summon the deceased through chants or offerings.

Christian Response: Communicating with the dead, whether through mediums or séances, is a form of necromancy and is strictly prohibited in Scripture (Deuteronomy 18:10-12). The Bible teaches that the dead cannot communicate with the living, and that attempting to do so opens believers to demonic influence (Luke 16:26). Christians are instructed to rely on God's Word for guidance, not the voices of the deceased (Hebrews 9:27, Matthew 22:32). This is, at times, an area of strong disagreement between Protestants and Catholics regarding the practice of praying to saints.

Pagan Practice: Use of "Third Eye" or "Chakra" Language
Description of the Practice: The use of "third eye" or "chakra" language is rooted in various Eastern spiritual traditions, particularly Hinduism, Buddhism, and New Age practices. In these systems, the third eye is often associated with spiritual awakening, inner vision, and heightened awareness, while chakras are believed to be energy centers in the body that affect physical, emotional, and spiritual well-being.

The third eye, thought to be in the middle of the forehead, is associated with spiritual awakening, inner vision, and heightened awareness. It is also linked to intuition, psychic abilities, and the capacity to see beyond the physical world.

The chakras are believed to be energy centers in the body that affect physical, emotional, and spiritual well-being. These energy centers correspond to different aspects of life and are connected to specific physical and emotional functions.

Christian Response: The Bible teaches that spiritual wisdom and guidance come from God alone, through the Holy Spirit. Passages like 1 Corinthians 2:14-16, Ephesians 1:17-18, and James 1:5 remind us that true understanding and insight are gifts from God, not something attained through mystical or occult practices. The pursuit of hidden knowledge or power through methods like the third eye or chakras is inconsistent with biblical teachings, which warn against engaging in practices associated with divination or sorcery (Deuteronomy 18:10-12).

Christian faith emphasizes the importance of seeking God through Christ, relying on the Holy Spirit for guidance, and worshiping God alone. Practices such as using the third eye or focusing on chakras shift attention away from the sufficiency of God's Word and His Spirit, potentially leading believers away from the path of true spiritual growth and reliance on Him.

SPIRITUAL SYNCRETISM

In evaluating the multitudinous practices of Paganism that have crept into the Christian ethos, it's worth recognizing the various formulations that have led to a spiraling devolution of orthodoxy among the faithful. Consider Sara Raztresen, a popular TikTok influencer and self-professed "Christian witch," who openly combines tarot cards with Christian devotions as a means of "conversing with God" through spiritual readings drawn from both sources. While some may be drawn to this alluring blend of spirituality, biblically grounded believers should immediately reject Raztresen's syncretistic faith, which mixes Christianity with overtly Pagan practices. Nevertheless, Raztresen's bold apostasy represents only a small, albeit radical, segment of Christians who, in name only, seek to redefine faith by blending the sacred with the occult. The real danger, however, lies in the fact that many Christians unknowingly and with less rebellious intentions embrace these Pagan practices to "reclaim" spiritual power, only to find themselves ensnared in unbiblical and occult influences.

For example, I recently attended an event where a Christian intercessor sought to pray for a national faith leader to "break the hexes" over their life. However, this intercessor, with the best of intentions, proposed an unorthodox method—using "deep prayer" to "cut the silver cord" that supposedly connected those attempting to use astral projection to physically attack the leader. Rather than simply calling on Jesus for grace and protection, or directly commanding any evil spirit to leave in Jesus' name, the intercessor intended to use customized incantations to undo these supposed hexes. Thankfully, the national faith leader, sensing a spiritual check, discerned the error and politely declined the practice.

Similarly, I received a report about a female minister who claims to use "astral projection"—which she calls "spirit travel"—to perform deliverance on other Christians. Through her teachings, this female minister is engaging in a practice that contradicts the biblical understanding of supernatural actions, which are always God-centered and divinely orchestrated. While the Bible does indeed speak of the supernatural ability to be physically moved by God's Spirit, astral projection relies on esoteric techniques and a belief in controlling one's spirit independently of God, opening the door to spiritual deception and occult influence.

For some, this may sound like splitting doctrinal hairs, but it's crucial to recognize that our power lies not in elaborate rituals or secret knowledge but in "Christ in us, the hope of glory" (Colossians 1:27). When we place our faith in secret disciplines and methods rather than in Christ Himself, we risk exchanging the Gospel's power for Pagan practices that pull us away from God's truth. For the early church, the emphasis was always on the authority of Christ alone—His death, resurrection, and indwelling Spirit—rather than on any external formula or mystical experience. Our hope and strength come from Christ living within us, not from ritualistic actions or mystical knowledge. In both instances, the minister's adoption of these practices (despite having the best of intentions) posed a risk to their spiritual integrity and the spiritual well-being of those they were ministering to.

By embracing a fusion of Christianity and Paganism, some believers, such as witnessed in the previous examples, begin to view their faith through a filter foreign to the Bible. It's a slow and often unintentional compromise, one that eventually dilutes the distinct, transformative power of the Gospel. Their faith becomes a mix of contradictory teachings rather than a pure devotion to Christ, and as they become more reliant on these "Christianized" Pagan practices, they grow less dependent on God's Spirit. It's a path that leads not toward deeper spiritual strength, but into a weakened faith unable to withstand the very cultural pressures we're called to resist.

To such individuals, Paul writes:

> *But I fear that, as the serpent deceived Eve by his cunning, your minds may be seduced from a sincere and pure devotion to Christ. For if a person comes and preaches another Jesus, whom we did not preach, or you receive a different spirit, which you had not received, or a different gospel, which you had not accepted, you put up with it splendidly!*[13]

Sadly, many will read these words and still find ways to justify their adaptations of Pagan practices alongside their Christian faith, claiming them to be spiritually permissible. This blending is not confined to personal spirituality but extends into political and social realms. Consider that 60% of mainline Protestant Christians in America support legal abortion[14]—a practice that, while sanitized by modern language, is fundamentally a socially acceptable form of child sacrifice. Despite its clear violation of Scripture and its condemnation throughout church history, it is often excused in the name of personal freedom or political expediency.

The justifications don't stop there. Many Christians rationalize their alignment with the meditative aspects of yoga, claiming it to be "just stretching," while ignoring its roots in Hindu spirituality. Others embrace crystals not for their aesthetic value but for their alleged "energetic properties," insisting they're merely engaging with "the science of it all." The excuses are endless: "It helps me focus," "It's just a tool," or "I don't believe in the spiritual elements—I'm just reclaiming it." Yet, no amount of explanation can erase the Pagan origins and unbiblical nature of these practices.

Tertullian's piercing question resounds across the centuries: "What indeed has Athens to do with Jerusalem? What concord is there between the Academy and the Church?"[15] His words warn us against mixing the wisdom of the world with the revelation of God. When Christians adopt Pagan practices and philosophies, whether out of ignorance or intent, they bring into the church what belongs outside it, diluting the Gospel and weakening their faith.

Such syncretism is not merely a harmless attempt to "reclaim" spiritual practices. It is a dangerous compromise that shifts the focus from Christ's sufficiency to human efforts, rituals, and objects. As Pastor Mark Driscoll said: "The result of syncretism is apostasy."[16] When we seek power or meaning outside the boundaries of Scripture, we not only betray our reliance on God but risk opening ourselves to spiritual deception. Nowhere has this happened more than in the widespread acceptance of LGBTQ+ ideology within the American church.

LGBTQ+: THE GREATEST PAGAN DECEPTION

According to Pew Research, 54% of Christians in the United States believe homosexuality should be accepted.[17] This majority sentiment reveals how deeply cultural narratives have influenced the church, with many believers prioritizing social acceptance over biblical fidelity. Instead of challenging the prevailing worldview with the unchanging truth of Scripture, these Christians have redefined their faith to align with society's expectations. Not only is it not uncommon to find mainstream churches proudly flying rainbow flags at full mast in major cities across the nation, but these pennants are also further bolstered by online queer "Christian" apologists offering robust "biblical" defenses of their orthodox defying stance. Content creators such as Rev. Brandon

Robertson and Rev. Kari A. Olson offer queer-affirming educational videos geared at normalizing LGBTQ+ lifestyles within the
framework of Christianity.

It's critically important that Christians recognize this infiltration of deceptive sexual morality, not as a progressive iteration of
Christianity "keeping up with the times," but as an onslaught of
Pagan ideology cloaked in Christian garb. This movement represents a calculated distortion of biblical orthodoxy, elevating
personal identity and cultural acceptance over God's unchanging
design for human sexuality. The rainbow flag—once a symbol of
God's covenant—is now reinterpreted as a banner for an ideology
that challenges the Creator's original intent. Such behavior can
only be called spiritual rebellion, as Scripture warns: "For rebellion is like the sin of divination, and defiance is like wickedness
and idolatry."[18] This is not merely a disagreement over doctrine; it
is the encroachment of ancient Pagan practices that exalt self-deification and rebellion against God's natural order.

Whereas Christianity has consistently rejected divergent
forms of sexuality within its moral framework, Paganism has not.
From the fertility cults of Baal and Ashtoreth,[19] which normalized
temple prostitution and ritualized sexual acts as acts of worship,
to the practices of the cult of Dionysus, where unrestrained passions and fluid identities were celebrated,[20] Pagan systems consistently embraced ideologies that challenged the moral boundaries
of biblical faith.

Several Pagan deities explicitly promoted or embodied
LGBTQ+ ideologies. The androgynous nature of Ishtar (Inanna),
the Mesopotamian goddess of love and war, is particularly striking; her worship involved rituals where gender roles were deliberately reversed, and male priests took on feminine personas
as they "changed themselves, making their maleness female-
ness."[21] Similarly, Hermaphroditus, the offspring of Hermes and

Aphrodite in Greek mythology, became a symbol of gender fluidity and the blending of male and female identities. Dionysus, the god of wine and revelry, was often portrayed in effeminate clothing and was associated with orgiastic rites that blurred traditional gender and sexual norms.[22] In Egypt, Hapi, the god of the Nile, was depicted as an intersex figure symbolizing fertility through the merging of masculine and feminine traits.

These deities and their associated cults celebrated what modern terminology would classify as LGBTQ+ expressions. Their ideologies, woven into their worship and cultural influence, exalted human autonomy and rejected the divine design of distinct, complementary male and female roles. By accepting similar beliefs and practices under the guise of Christian love and inclusivity, the church risks repeating the errors of Israel, which often strayed into idolatry by embracing the surrounding nations' gods and their associated sexual ethics.

King Solomon loved many foreign women in addition to Pharoah's daughter: Moabite, Edomite, Sidonian, and Hittite women from the nations about which the Lord had told the Israelites, "You must not intermarry with them, and they must not intermarry with you, because they will turn your heart away to follow their gods." To these women, Solomon was deeply attached in love. He had seven hundred wives who were princesses and three hundred who were concubines, and they turned his heart away. When Solomon was old, his wives turned his heart away to follow other gods. He was not wholeheartedly devoted to the Lord his God, as his father David had been. Solomon followed Ashtoreth, the goddess of the Sidonians, and Milcom, the abhorrent idol of the Ammonites. Solomon did what was evil in the Lord's sight, and unlike his father David, he did not remain loyal to the Lord.[23]

Solomon's story highlights how his marriages to foreign women, despite God's command to avoid such unions, ultimately turned his heart away from the Lord. These attachments—rooted in love and affection—led him to embrace the gods and sexual ethics of foreign nations, fundamentally altering his relationship with God.

Similarly, many Christians today, deeply attached to family members who identify as LGBTQ+, are being influenced to soften or abandon traditional biblical views on sexuality. The cultural pressure to accept LGBTQ+ ideology, especially when it involves close family members, mirrors Solomon's gradual but devastating departure from biblical fidelity. This acceptance is often framed under the guise of love, inclusion, and tolerance, much like Solomon's initial intentions were likely not malicious but rooted in his affection for his wives. But just as Solomon's tolerance for foreign gods ultimately led to idolatry, the church today risks embracing ideologies that distort God's design for human sexuality.

PRESSED ON EVERY SIDE

As we have seen, the creeping influence of Paganism within the church—from obvious Pagan practices, such as witchcraft, crystals, and tarot cards, to more subtle infiltrations, like the Enneagram, spiritual syncretism, and LGBTQ+ ideology—has led to a significant departure from orthodox Christian teachings. The embrace of these ideas is not just a matter of individual belief; it represents a broader shift in the church's alignment with cultural trends that are at odds with the foundational principles of Christianity. These compromises, however well-intentioned, expose a troubling shift where the church is more concerned with fitting in than standing firm in the truth of Scripture. This embrace of cultural ideologies has weakened the Gospel, transforming the faith into a more palatable version of Christianity that aligns with worldly values rather than biblical ones.

As the church faces increasing pressure to conform to societal norms, it is no surprise that many Christians are feeling the weight of the battle for the soul of the church. The rise of secular ideologies, from the LGBTQ+ movement to the worship of self, has left the church at a crossroads. The temptation to solve this crisis by returning to a more forceful approach, especially after the overwhelming victory of President Trump in 2024, is gaining traction among some believers. This desire to fight back against secularism, though understandable, risks taking the church further away from its true mission of spreading the Gospel. The growing cultural and philosophical clashes between Christianity and secular ideologies demand not only a response but also a careful reconsideration of how Christians should engage in the public sphere without compromising their faith.

In the coming chapter, we will explore the mounting challenges and criticisms the church faces today, as well as the broader cultural climate that has contributed to the perceived decline of Christianity. The temptation to return to a more militant version of Christianity may seem appealing to some, but we must examine the consequences of such an approach and whether it truly reflects Christ's call to love and serve than to dominate or coerce. The church is indeed on trial, but it is not simply under attack from external forces—there is a deeper internal reckoning that must take place if it is to remain faithful to its mission in a rapidly changing world.

SEVEN

THE CHURCH
ON TRIAL

JESUS: THE IMMORAL ONE

While the church has spent the better part of half a century delighting in the grand spectacle of evangelistic crusades, the renaissance of Christian music and arts, and the towering ambitions of the megachurch movement, a quieter yet more sinister procession has been assembling in the shadows. While we have marched triumphantly in the glow of our achievements, the ancient enemies of the faith have not been idle. Like wolves gathering on the distant hills, they have been forming ranks, sharpening their claws, and renewing their age-old critique of Christianity. It seems, as ever, that while the saints were singing, the demons were scheming.

Their scheming has taken on new yet strangely familiar forms, weaving the threads of deconstructionism and Pagan revivalism into a tapestry of doubt and accusation against the Christian faith. Deconstructionism seeks to unravel the very fabric of belief, leaving Christians questioning not only the traditions they hold dear but also the foundational truths upon which their faith rests. Meanwhile, the Pagan revival dresses up timeworn heresies in modern garb, seducing a now doubt-filled restless generation with promises of self-made spirituality and cosmic harmony—carefully curated to rack up likes on Instagram for a culture craving meaning. Together, these forces conspire to present Christianity not as the bedrock of civilization but as an outdated antique, its moral authority questioned, its claims to truth ridiculed, and its adherents painted as oppressive taskmasters of a bygone age.

Reigniting old accusations against the Christian faith, Pagans and deconstructionists have unearthed an arsenal of criticism, accusing believers of historical crimes—colonialism, patriarchy, and cultural oppression. They wield these charges not only to tarnish Christianity's past but to undermine its present influence. Alongside these claims, they seek to discredit the Scriptures, casting doubt on their authority and divine inspiration, while amplifying the failings of prominent faith leaders as evidence of pervasive hypocrisy. In this narrative, orthodox Christianity is recast not as the faith that frees the captive and redeems the broken but as a system of domination, an oppressive force that stifles liberation rather than fosters it.

As Carl R. Trueman observes, many of these claims intensified "in the aftermath of the Trump presidency" when "it became routine to hear religious conservatives in general, and evangelical Christians in particular, decried as representing a threat to civil society."[1]

Examples of such rhetoric include:

- "The very heart of American Christianity is oppression."[2]
- "Religion is undoubtedly a divisive force."[3]
- "If you can convince the masses that a Rabbi from 2,000 years ago was crucified and came back from the dead then you can convince them to conquer, enslave, and slaughter in 'His' name."[4]
- "Morality doesn't stem from Christianity! In fact, most of our moral code stems from Pre-Christian times, and the Bible is full of immoral scenes."[5]
- "Racism among white Christians is higher than among the nonreligious."[6]

Accusations such as these reflect not merely individual grievances but the cumulative effect of centuries of shifting thought
patterns that have moved Western culture away from its Christian
foundations. Trueman describes this process as "de-Christianiz-
ing,"[7] and he notes that "the opposition is likely better informed
and more proactive than in the ancient church."[8] This "better
informed"[9] drift began in the Enlightenment[10] where reason was
elevated as the primary arbiter of truth and human autonomy
was prioritized over divine authority. Over time, these philosophical shifts gave rise to a fragmented worldview, where the
Christian narrative of creation, fall, redemption, and restoration
was increasingly replaced by relativism, skepticism, and alternative spiritualities, that is to say, postmodernism.

UNDERSTANDING THE BACKLASH

In his book *Explaining Postmodernism*, Stephen R. C. Hicks writes,
"Postmodernism is the end result of the Counter-Enlightenment
inaugurated" by philosopher Immanuel Kant. This shift, as Hicks
explains, traces its roots to Kant's challenge to the Enlightenment's
reliance on reason and objective truth. By arguing that human
knowledge is confined to subjective perceptions of reality (phenomena) and cannot truly access the world as it is (noumena),
Kant laid the philosophical foundation for the skepticism and relativism that would come to define postmodernism.

This philosophical upheaval not only dismantled confidence
in absolute truths but also opened the door to diverse spiritual
frameworks, including the resurgence of ancient Pagan ideologies. The pluralistic and experiential worldview of Paganism
aligned seamlessly with postmodernism's rejection of universal
truths—it was a marriage made in . . . well, not Heaven, I suppose.

Whereas Christianity offers a singular, objective moral and metaphysical framework grounded in divine revelation, whereas postmodernism and Pagan revivalism embrace a fragmented, personalized spirituality untethered from absolute authority. Trueman exemplifies that this is because:

> *The notion of a sacred order has been largely abandoned. The fear of theocracy and the demands of pluralism that mark our societies, in addition to the collapse of the authority of traditional religious institutions, have combined to make appeals to any kind of sacred order implausible and even unacceptable. . . . As with the collapse of the authority of church, nation, and family, this creates a vacuum of moral authority that is filled with the competing voices of a myriad of new identities and no objective way of adjudicating between them.*[11]

The cultural shift that followed this "vacuum of moral authority"[12] is crucial to understanding the backlash against Christianity today. As Trueman points out, the confusion of "competing voices" has instilled a skepticism within postmodernism toward grand narratives and universal truths, which has fostered an environment where Christianity's moral authority and truth claims are not only questioned but actively rejected, often met with suspicion, misrepresentation, and criticism. Furthermore, the Pagan ideas reemerging to fill the vacuum of moral authority—cloaked in the language of liberation and progress—present a compelling alternative to what many critics perceive as the oppressive metanarrative of Christianity.

These attacks, primed and loaded by a dramatic cultural flux, are not merely a reaction to the historical failings of God's people but are rooted in the broader philosophical currents that have shaped our modern worldview. As philosophical skepticism undermines Christian truths on a macro scale, it simultaneously fuels a more focused assault on the faith, manifesting in three primary critiques:

- *The Goodness of God.* Critics often challenge the morality of God, pointing to specific passages in Scripture or historical events they interpret as evidence of divine cruelty, injustice, or contradiction.
- *The Church's Role in Justice.* Accusations of patriarchy, systemic oppression, and complicity in injustice are commonly directed at the church, framing it not as a force for liberation but as a defender of entrenched power structures.
- *Christianity's Exclusivity.* The faith's doctrines on salvation, truth, and morality—particularly in relation to gender, sexuality, and the doctrine of Hell—are criticized as narrow and too exclusionary for an inclusive and relativistic world.

If Christians are to respond to these critiques, we must understand and unpack the specific charges against the faith and examine how and why they resonate in a society increasingly shaped by postmodern relativism, Woke buzzwords, and neo-Pagan ideals. Perhaps only then will we be able to provide a defense that is not only intellectually sound but rooted in the timeless truth of the Gospel. It is in this enduring truth that we find the strength to stand firm, as the church has always done, against the tide of skepticism and opposition.

UNDERSTANDING THE THREE CRITIQUES

The judgment of God is no modern innovation. It is as old as humanity itself, as ancient as the first whisper of rebellion in the Garden of Eden. When Adam and Eve stood before the Tree of the Knowledge of Good and Evil in Genesis 3, they did not merely disobey God's command—they judged it. They weighed His wisdom in the balance of their own desires and declared Him lacking. "Did God really say?"[13] was not just a question; it was an accusation, a seed of doubt that grew into outright defiance.

Since that moment, humanity has been in the business of putting God on trial. From the murmuring Israelites in the wilderness[14] to Job's three friends who misrepresented God's justice,[15] the impulse to question, accuse, and reject divine authority has been a recurring theme. At its core, it's the story of humanity's pride: a creature shaking its fist at its Creator, convinced it could do better.

Today, this tendency takes on new forms, but its heart remains unchanged. Through the lens of modern skepticism, postmodern relativism, and the revival of Pagan practices, humanity continues to pass judgment on God, His Church, and His truth. These critiques are not new; they are reverberations of the same serpent's lie: "You will be like God."[16]

As we examine the three primary critiques of Christianity— attacks on the goodness of God, the Church's role in justice, and the exclusivity of the Gospel—we see that they are not merely analytical arguments against the faith, but deeply spiritual rebellions. They are attempts to remake God in the image of the culture and to subject divine truth to human judgment. But as we confront these accusations, we are reminded that the Christian faith has endured such challenges before, not by retreating or capitulating, but by standing firm in the unchanging truth of the Gospel.

Let's look at these critiques more closely, before exploring the essential Christian response in the next chapter.

THE GOODNESS OF GOD

The first and most common accusation, often referred to as the "problem of evil," has troubled philosophers and theologians for centuries: "If God is good, why do bad things happen?"[17] Critics point to the global flood in Genesis, the fiery judgment on Sodom and Gomorrah, or the conquest of Canaan as if each story were a smoking gun in the hands of a celestial tyrant. They reason, "Why do the innocent suffer? Why are children born into war zones, like Ukraine or Gaza, or afflicted by disease? Why do earthquakes devastate entire villages, and tsunamis erase miles of coastline? Surely, a good God would not permit such horrors." And on the argument goes.

From their vantage point, either God can stop the atrocities but chooses not to, thus casting doubts on His goodness, or He is willing to intervene but is powerless to do so, thereby revealing limitations in His power. Worst yet, the accusations compound by not only questioning God's limitations but accusing Him (or at least the idea of Him) directly of being the source of evil itself.

"He made us this way, with desires and weaknesses, placed us in a world teeming with temptation, and then judges us for the very faults He hardwired into us," the critics will say. The doctrine of eternal damnation fuels this fire. How can a God who calls Himself love create a world where His own children, fashioned in His image, might end up in eternal torment all because of desires that He gave them?

British evolutionary biologist and outspoken atheist Richard Dawkins outlines the prosecution's position that "the central doctrine of Christianity,"[18] what he describes as the "atonement for original sin,"[19] is "morally obnoxious."[20] Offering a further explanation, Dawkins adds, "What kind of ethical philosophy is it that condemns every child, even before it is born, to inherit the sin of a remote ancestor?"[21] Atheist and self-proclaimed "contrarian"[22] Christopher Hitchens, agrees adding:

> *Once again we have a father demonstrating love by subjecting a son to death by torture, but this time the father is not trying to impress god. He is god, and he is trying to impress humans. Ask yourself the question: how moral is the following? I am told of a human sacrifice that took place 2,000 years ago, without my wishing it and in circumstances so ghastly that, had I been present and in possession of any influence, I would have been duty-bound to try and stop it. In consequence of this murder, my own manifold sins are forgiven me, and I may hope to enjoy everlasting life.*[23]

While it's easy as a Christian to dismiss Dawkins and Hitchens, if we expect to win people from the grips of Pagan revivalism and the deep, dark hole of atheistic despair, these claims must be heard, as they represent the sentiments of a growing population who are increasingly skeptical of traditional Christian teachings. The accusation is not just a philosophical inquiry—it is a challenge to the very nature of God's justice and love. The questions are real, and they resonate deeply within a culture that struggles to reconcile the existence of suffering with the idea of a benevolent Creator.

THE CHURCH'S ROLE IN JUSTICE

While the problem of evil has long been a theological conundrum, accusations against God regarding issues of justice represent a more modern conversation—one deeply influenced by Marxist thought and contemporary Woke ideologies. Often, these criticisms view historical events and contemporary issues, through a critical lens, where the church is seen as either complicit in injustice or actively perpetuating harmful systems. One recent post shared by X user (ironically, named Lilith) who describes herself as a "Demon and atheist from the depths of Hell," summarizes several common charges made against Christianity, including:[24]

- Religious wars and persecution
- Colonialism and forced conversions
- Opposition to science (e.g., Galileo)
- Social oppression (slavery, patriarchy, anti-LGBTQ+)
- Suppression of other beliefs
- Moral control and reproductive rights limits
- Guilt and fear teachings

Hitchens, among his other grievances, agrees with Lilith's premise, blaming the church for similar charges, including its "historic responsibility for the Crusades"[25] and its "combat against science and reason."[26] Like many of today's critics, Hitchens and the X user Lilith, argue that from the Crusades to the Inquisition, the church has often been a force for violence and suppression, justifying wars, persecutions, and forced conversions as part of its mission.

These accusations against the church, while often exaggerated or rooted in misunderstanding, reflect a growing sentiment of disillusionment with Christianity's historical and cultural influence.

Critics frame the church as a bastion of oppression rather than a beacon of hope, portraying it as a driving force behind centuries of injustice and a hindrance to progress in the modern world. Whether the charges concern violence, coercion, or the imposition of moral norms, they demand an answer—not merely for the sake of rebuttal, but to demonstrate how the church, at its best, seeks to embody the justice, mercy, and truth of the God it professes to serve.

CHRISTIANITY'S EXCLUSIVITY

The third, and perhaps most divisive, critique of Christianity today is its perceived exclusivity. In a world shaped by Diversity, Equity and Inclusion, Critical Race Theory, and LGBTQ+ indoctrination, Christianity's claims to be the one true path to salvation and its teachings on morality and truth are increasingly seen as narrow and intolerant. So much so that atheists, like Dawkins, described conservative evangelicals as "the American Taliban,"[27] citing strong statements against homosexuality from both Liberty University founder Jerry Falwell and longtime host of *The 700 Club* Pat Robertson as proof of what he calls Christians' "religious absolutism."[28]

The critique of Christianity's exclusivity often arises from its central claim that salvation comes only through faith in Jesus Christ. As revealed in the Apostle Peter's proclamation, "There is salvation in no one else, for there is no other name under heaven given to people by which we must be saved."[29] This assertion stands in bold opposition to the prevailing cultural emphasis on inclusivity, which boasts multiple paths to the divine. Atheists like Dawkins have amplified this narrative by dishonestly labeling conservative evangelicals, equating their unwavering moral convictions with religious extremism. Consequently, Christianity's "one-way" doctrine and its insistence on absolute truth are frequently accused of being intolerant and oppressive in a society that demands diverse perspectives.

This tension is further exacerbated by the doctrine of Hell, which many view as an unloving and punitive construct. Critics ask, "How can a faith that professes to love all people condemn anyone to eternal torment for failing to believe in its narrow path to salvation?" From this perspective, Christianity is not seen as a faith of liberation but as a system of control, demanding conformity under the threat of eternal punishment.

In all three critiques—whether of God's goodness, the church's role in justice, or Christianity's exclusivity—the heart of the issue remains the same: Humanity desires to define truth, morality, and justice on its own terms. These critiques are not mere ideological challenges but spiritual rebellions. They are the same original questions that echo from the Garden of Eden, rephrased in modern language, but fundamentally unchanged. And just as humanity sided with the devil and stood in judgment of God from the very beginning, it continues to do so today by questioning, accusing, and rejecting divine authority.

In the next chapter, we will explore these critiques further to test their substance. While the charges against God may seem damning at first glance, the deeper we look, the more the story begins to change, but first, we will require a roadmap on how to deal with them.

MORAL ACCUSATIONS

Part of what makes these accusations so disheartening is their veneer of plausibility. They draw from a mixture of genuine historical missteps and outright distortions, often magnified by a culture eager to find fault with Christianity. Yes, Christians have made errors throughout history—some grievous and undeniable—but these failings are human, not divine, and stand in stark contrast to the redemptive truth of the Gospel. Yet, critics seize upon these missteps, distorting them into sweeping indictments of the faith itself. They claim that Paul was sexist,[30] the Bible is homophobic, or Christianity has always been a tool of oppression. These accusations are rooted not in an honest reading of Scripture or history, but in a deliberate attempt to undermine the church's moral authority.

And therein lies the deeper tactic: By dismantling the moral standing of Christianity, critics aim to bypass Jesus entirely. If the church is seen as morally bankrupt, then the teachings of Jesus are discredited by association. Worse still, if Jesus Himself can be framed as immoral—whether through misrepresentations of His teachings or the actions of His followers—then His lordship is nullified. After all, a Lord who is not moral cannot be the Lord at all. In this framework, critics no longer even need to grapple with the resurrection or the claims of Jesus' divinity. If His moral authority can be undermined, the heart of the faith collapses, and Christianity is dismissed without ever addressing its central truth claims.

This tactic paints believers not merely as flawed—something Scripture itself acknowledges about all humanity—but as part of an ongoing systemic framework of oppression and bigotry. Of course, this is not the first time Christianity has stood accused in the court of public opinion. These critiques, while completely different from the "holier-than-thou" rhetoric against the church of yesteryear, are eerily familiar to the accusations levied against the early church. The brilliant Carl R. Trueman describes the church's current predicament this way:

> If we are to find a precedent for our times, I believe that we must go further back in time, to the second century and the immediately post-apostolic church. There, Christianity was a little-understood, despised, marginal sect. It was suspected of being immoral and seditious. Eating the body and blood of their god and calling each other "brother" and "sister" even when married made Christians and Christianity sound highly dubious to outsiders. And the claim that "Jesus is Lord!" was on the surface a pledge of loyalty that derogated from that owed to Caesar. That is much like the situation of the church today. For example, we are considered irrational bigots for our stance on gay marriage. In the aftermath of the Trump presidency, it has become routine to hear religious conservatives in general, and evangelical Christians in particular, decried as representing a threat to civil society. Like our spiritual ancestors in the second century, we too are deemed immoral and seditious.[31]

To combat such claims, we can't seek answers from previous decades when Christianity enjoyed cultural dominance, nor can we rely solely on modern apologetics shaped by relative comfort. Instead, we must look back to the days of the early church itself—a time when Christians faced a far more hostile culture. In fact, one man stood firm in the face of accusations far graver than those we endure today. He offered thoughtful, reasoned defenses that addressed misunderstandings, corrected false narratives, and pointed to the transformative power of the Gospel.

By examining his approach, we gain not only a blueprint for defending our faith but also a renewed confidence in the enduring truth of Christianity—a faith that has weathered storms far greater than the ones we face today. This hero of the faith is Justin Martyr and his example stands as a beacon of light for Christians navigating a culture eager to dismiss their beliefs.

Let's delve into the challenges Justin Martyr confronted and explore how his courage and theological rigor offer timeless lessons for addressing the critiques of our own day.

EARLY APOLOGIES

By the mere application of a name, nothing is decided, either good or evil, apart from the actions implied in the name; and indeed, so far at least as one may judge from the name we are accused of, we are the most excellent people. But as we do not think it just to beg to be acquitted on account of the name, if we be convicted as evildoers, so, on the other hand, if we be found to have committed no offense, either in the matter of thus naming ourselves, or of our conduct as citizens, it is your part very earnestly to guard against incurring just punishment, by unjustly punishing those who are not convicted. . . . For we are accused of being Christians, and to hate what is excellent is unjust.[32]

These stirring words from Justin Martyr's *First Apology* are both a plea and a paradox—a call for justice in a world that so often distorts it. Justin lived in an age that was remarkably inventive in its accusations. The Roman Empire, despite its pantheon of gods, gilded temples, and stern-faced statues of emperors, feared the Christians not for their crimes but for their virtues.

To be a Christian in the second century was to live under a banner of scandal. You could be accused of atheism for rejecting the gods,[33] of treason for refusing to bow to Caesar,[34] or of immorality for gathering in secret to break bread.[35] It was as though the very brightness of Christian hope cast an unnerving shadow over the dimly lit idols of the empire.

Justin Martyr, philosopher and apologist, was not content to let these accusations go unanswered. He saw the absurdity in a society that charged Christians with "atheism" for worshiping the unseen God while others venerated statues of stone and bronze. He recognized the irony in being accused of cannibalism by those who staged blood-soaked gladiatorial games for entertainment. And he dared to suggest that the Christians—those misunderstood followers of Christ—might just be the most excellent people the empire had yet produced.

But Justin did more than defend. He attacked—not with violence but with the sharp blade of reason. To those who called Christians a threat to Rome, he replied that the Gospel was the true foundation of justice, a morality higher than the whims of emperors or the machinations of priests. Where Rome offered bread and circuses, Christianity offered the bread of life.

Justin's *First Apology*, written to Emperor Antoninus Pius, was not a groveling appeal for tolerance. It was a bold declaration of truth. It demanded that Christianity be judged not by its enemies' slander but by its fruits—fruits that were, in Justin's words, "the most excellent." His *Second Apology*, written to defend persecuted believers, pressed even further, revealing the moral and philosophical emptiness of Paganism, compared to the radiant coherence of Christ's teachings.

Demonstrating both clarity of thought and compassion, Justin boldly reasoned:

Wherefore we demand that the deeds of all those who are
accused to you be judged, in order that each one who is
convicted may be punished as an evil-doer, and not as a
Christian; and if it is clear that anyone is blameless, that
he may be acquitted, since by the mere fact of his being a
Christian he does no wrong. For we will not require that you
punish our accusers; they being sufficiently punished by their
present wickedness and ignorance of what is right.[36]

This was no ordinary plea for justice; it was a direct challenge
to an empire blinded by its own corruption, but Justin didn't stop
there. He confronted the folly of idol worship with unflinching
precision, declaring:

And neither do we honor with many sacrifices and garlands
of flowers such deities as men have formed and set in shrines
and called gods; since we see that these are soulless and dead,
and have not the form of God, but have the names and forms
of those wicked demons which have appeared.[37]

And again, bringing his argument full circle, Justin built
upon his claim that Christians are the "most excellent people,"[38]
asserting:

And more than all other men are we your helpers and allies
in promoting peace, seeing that we hold this view, that it is
alike impossible for the wicked, the covetous, the conspirator,
and for the virtuous, to escape the notice of God, and that
each man goes to everlasting punishment or salvation
according to the value of his actions. For if all men knew this,
no one would choose wickedness even for a little, knowing
that he goes to the everlasting punishment of fire; but would
by all means restrain himself, and adorn himself with virtue,

that he might obtain the good gifts of God, and escape
punishments.[39]

What made early "Greek Apologists" like Justin so unique
when compared to apologists of today was how they acted toward
rulers of the Roman Empire, according to Trueman. Trueman
continued:

> *They did not spend their time denouncing the evils of the*
> *emperor and his court. Rather, they argued positively that*
> *Christians made the best citizens, the best parents, the best*
> *servants, the best neighbors, the best employees, and that they*
> *should thus be left alone and allowed to carry on with their*
> *day-to-day lives without being harassed by the authorities. Of*
> *course, there were limits to what they could do to participate*
> *in civic life: if asked to sacrifice to the emperor as to a god,*
> *they would have to refuse, but beyond such demands, they*
> *could be good members of the Roman community.*[40]

While Justin may have approached it with respect, as Trueman
suggests, there is no denying that his defense of the Christian
faith not only confronted the Roman Empire's distorted view of
Christians but also struck at the very core of Pagan philosophy. It
was a daring polemic, positioning Christianity not as something
to be merely tolerated, but as a faith and a community vital to the
health and prosperity of the city-state. His words rang with an
unwavering conviction, illuminating the darkness of his era—an
era bent on snuffing out the light of Christ through slander and
persecution.

Today, we find ourselves in a strikingly similar tempest. The
church is vilified, the Christian faith misunderstood, and the
name of Christ maligned under the banners of modern ideologies.

The accusations may have changed their terminology—"bigot" replacing "atheist," "oppressor" standing in for "traitor"—but the underlying animosity remains the same.

In a similar situation in his day, Justin did not respond with despair or retreat. Instead, he stood firm, not only exposing the incoherence of the culture that opposed his faith but also "presenting it [the opposing culture] with another culture."[41] His example challenges us to do the same—not by merely replicating his arguments, but by crafting a new apology that speaks to our unique challenges. We must confront the accusations of our time—whether they come in the form of Woke ideologies, Pagan revivalism, or moral relativism—with the same boldness and clarity that Justin exhibited. And more than just defending our faith, we must offer the world a compelling and clear reason to choose the Christian faith once again.

Armed with this mindset, Justin becomes not only a historical figure but a guide. His world was a storm of Paganism, persecution, and philosophical confusion. In that storm, he stood, not with a sword but with a pen, proving that the truth of Christ was more compelling than the myths of the gods and the ambitions of emperors. What he wrote nearly two millennia ago still speaks, not because it was clever, but because it was true. And truth, as Justin well knew, is the most excellent defense of all.

As we consider the task before us, we must ask: What would a modern apology for the Christian faith look like? How can we, in the spirit of Justin, boldly defend the faith in a world eager to dismiss it? These are the questions we will explore in the next chapter, as we seek to craft a defense that not only withstands the critiques of our age but will shine as a city on a hill for generations to come.

EIGHT

A NEW
APOLOGETIC

AMERICA NEEDS A NEW APOLOGY

When shaping a new theological apology* in the face of a Pagan resurgence, it's important to remember that the goal is twofold. First, we must defend the faith against false accusations, and second, we must win over those who oppose it with the clear truth of the Gospel. The Apostle Paul embodied this sentiment toward Festus, the Roman governor of Judea and King Agrippa, when he confessed, "I wish before God that whether easily or with difficulty, not only you but all who listen to me today might become as I am—except for these chains."[1] In this same evangelistic spirit, Justin Martyr wrote to Emperor Antoninus Pius, and his sons Marcus Aurelius and Lucius, in his *First Apology*:

> For we have come, not to flatter you by this writing, nor
> please you by our address, but to beg that you pass judgment,
> after an accurate and searching investigation, not flattered
> by prejudice or by a desire of pleasing superstitious men, nor

---

* In Christian philosophy, the term "apology" does not refer to an expression of regret or sorrow but rather to a reasoned defense or justification of the Christian faith. The term comes from the Greek word *apologia*, meaning a verbal defense or speech in defense of one's beliefs. Early Christian apologists, such as Justin Martyr and Tertullian, wrote works to defend Christianity against criticism and to explain its doctrines to non-believers.

*induced by irrational impulse or evil rumors which have
long been prevalent, to give a decision which will prove to be
against yourselves. For as for us, we reckon that no evil can
be done us, unless we be convicted as evil-doers or be proved
to be wicked men; and you, you can kill, but not hurt us.*

It is this unflinching commitment to truth, driven by the love of Christ, in the face of Pagan cultures that binds the testimonies of Paul and Justin together. Both men understood that the defense of the Gospel was not a mere mental exercise nor a public relations campaign. For these two champions of the faith, it was an act of spiritual warfare, waged not with the weapons of the world but with the armor of God and the sword of the Spirit. Paul stood before rulers with chains on his wrists, and Justin stood before an empire with death on the horizon. Yet, neither wavered, because their hope was not in the favor of men but in the eternal promise of Christ. They spoke not to appease but to convict, not to win arguments but to win souls.

And so, when crafting a defense of the faith today, we must take a page from their example: Speak with clarity and courage, reject flattery and fear, and remember always that our goal is not victory in debate but the transformation of hearts. And fortunately, in the view of modern apologist William Lane Craig, significant opportunities exist to do just that:

*We are living at a time when Christian philosophy is
experiencing a veritable renaissance, reinvigorating natural
theology, at a time when science is more open to the existence
of a transcendent Creator and Designer of the cosmos than
at any time in recent memory.*[2]

According to the *Wall Street Journal*, Craig might be onto something. A recent report shows a "22% jump in Bible sales"[3] in 2024. The increased interest in the Good Book, it appears, was largely fueled by Gen Z, which John Plake, chief program officer at the American Bible Society, describes as "a bright hope for us as a young generation of American adults,"[4] as nearly half of the generation has said "the Bible has transformed their lives."[5]

Adding to the optimism these stats provide are recent celebrity conversions, including Russell Brand,[6] Lola Sheen,[7] Shia LaBeouf,[8] and the baptism and pastoral ordination of Denzel Washington.[9] These conversions are further illuminated by the evidence of ongoing Christian resurgence throughout the United States, such as the 2023 revival at Asbury University,[10] the two-day mass baptism event, known as "Baptize California," which led to over 12,000 people being baptized in the state, including 6,000 individuals in one day at Huntington Beach,[11] and recent "athletes from a host of teams"[12] using press conferences to testify about Jesus.

While these stories and statistics provide reason for encouragement, we must not forget that our nation has been ravaged for years by Pagan ideology disguised as Woke thought—a force that, despite the best efforts of many, will not simply fade away overnight. From the gender indoctrination of our children in schools to the rise of perverse sexual expressions like "throuples,"[13] from national leaders bowing the knee to criminals as if they were deities[14] to the support of a death cult that glorifies the killing of innocent children[15]—America needs a new apology for the Christian faith!

This new apology, if successful, must do more than push back against the false ideologies that have taken root in our culture. It must answer the hard questions and rebuttals of the previous chapters. It must affirm the unshakable goodness of God, articulate a biblical response to issues of injustice, and boldly defend the exclusivity of the Gospel. And it must do all of this without compromise—without watering down the truth of Scripture or succumbing to the pressures of a nation intent on its own moral decline.

WITHOUT EXCUSE

This may sound like a tall order, but fortunately, as believers, we can rest assured that all men, regardless of what they may claim, at one time or another, possessed a knowledge of God. That might seem hard to believe while watching Charlie Kirk or Cliffe Knechtle get lectured by blue-haired gender studies majors—people who reject absolute truth with the same breath they use to declare their preferred pronouns sacred, and their feelings infallible. But Paul leaves no room for ambiguity in Romans:

> Since what can be known about God is evident among
> them, because God has shown it to them. For His invisible
> attributes, that is, His eternal power and divine nature,
> have been clearly seen since the creation of the world, being
> understood through what He has made. As a result, people
> are without excuse. For though they knew God, they did not
> glorify Him as God or show gratitude. Instead, their thinking
> became worthless, and their senseless hearts were darkened.[16]

Adding to this biblical truth, Athanasius, an early Christian bishop and theologian who also understood the inherent awareness of God present in every soul, states:

> And let not the Greeks, who worship idols, make excuses, nor
> let anyone else simply deceive himself, professing to have no
> such road and therefore finding a pretext for his godliness.

For we all have set foot upon it, and have it, even if not all
are willing to travel by it, but rather to swerve from it and
go wrong; because of the pleasures of life which attract them
from without. And if one were to ask, what road is this? I say
that it is the soul of each one of us, and the intelligence which
resides there. For by it alone can God be contemplated and
perceived.

Athanasius emphasizes that, no matter the cultural confusion or ideological noise, every person possesses the capacity to
know God—including those blue-haired gender studies majors—
because He has etched this knowledge into the very fabric of the
soul through the innate, God-given intelligence He has provided.

Yet, it's no surprise that those who have rejected God often
perceive Him as being void of goodness or lacking in some capacity. As the Bible describes in Ephesians 2:3 (CSB), they are "by
nature children under wrath." These individuals experience only
the wrath of God because they have previously rejected His goodness, the very essence of His nature. They have turned away from
His calling and the invitation to a relationship, which leaves them
only to encounter the consequences of their rebellion. This rejection leads them to a distorted view of God—one in which His
wrath is the only aspect they can experience because they refuse
to embrace His loving kindness, which is always extended to those
who turn toward Him. As the prophet Isaiah proclaims: "Let the
wicked one abandon his way and the sinful one his thoughts; let
him return to the Lord, so he may have compassion on him, and
to our God, for he will freely forgive."[17]

Thus, it's crucial to understand that the innate knowledge
of God that exists within every human being is not something
that can be entirely suppressed. It can be ignored, denied, or even
twisted into something else, but it cannot be erased. When we

present the Gospel, we are not introducing something foreign or unknown to the human heart. Instead, we are drawing out what has always been there—the call of God to return to Him and to acknowledge the truth that has been revealed to all through creation, which invites each person into the transformative relationship He offers.

We see this even among those who chase after Paganism, witchcraft, or Earth worship as supposed alternatives to Christ. They reject Him, yet they cannot help but borrow from Him—fashioning their own versions of justice, morality, and even divine order, unwittingly bearing witness to the very God they deny. Their rebellion is not evidence of God's absence but of their refusal to surrender to the truth they cannot escape.

For today's spiritually confused generation, however, this innate knowledge of God is often buried beneath layers of false ideology casting Him as distant, indifferent, or even oppressive. In a culture shaped by secularism and counterfeit spiritualities, many resist the God of Scripture—not because they truly know Him, but because they have embraced a distorted view of His character. They mistake His justice for harshness, His holiness for intolerance, and His commands for burdens rather than blessings. But this is precisely why the church must recover and proclaim a fuller, richer understanding of God's goodness—a goodness that is neither passive nor permissive but powerful, just, and redemptive. If we fail to do so, we leave the culture to define Him by its misguided assumptions (as described throughout this book) rather than by the truth He has revealed.

For many, even Christians themselves, the idea of a good God is obscured by spiritual misconceptions, painful experiences, and perverted misrepresentations of God's truth—both from secular influences and from erroneous interpretations within the church itself. For those who have become disillusioned—often due to negative experiences with church or pastoral figures—the rejection of God frequently begins with the rejection of His goodness. In these cases, apologetics alone will not suffice. Even if we can prove God's existence, their perception of His inherent flaws will continue to block them from seeking any relationship with Him.

Thus, when presented with alternative Pagan practices that promise many of the same benefits as Christianity—such as spiritual insight, inner peace, or a sense of purpose—but without the past pain attached to the personal nature or personhood of the living God, they are easily drawn in. These alternatives often claim to offer wisdom, transcendence, and divine connection, yet they strip away not only the object of their offense but the defining reality of true faith as well: The goodness of God Himself. These Pagan spiritual systems may provide a fleeting sense of empowerment or control, but they cannot satisfy the deepest human longing. That longing can only be fulfilled by the goodness of the God who created us.

To overcome this, false beliefs about God's goodness must be dismantled and replaced with the truth of Scripture. As 2 Corinthians 10:4-5 (CSB) states:

> *Since the weapons of our warfare are not of the flesh, but are powerful through God for the demolition of strongholds, we demolish arguments and every proud thing that is raised up against the knowledge of God, and we take every thought captive to obey Christ.*[18]

Only by confronting and dismantling these false perceptions, and replacing them with biblical truth, can the fullness of God's goodness be revealed and embraced.

IS THE CHRISTIAN GOD REALLY GOOD?

The rise of deconstructionism and the allure of neo-Pagan practices are not being driven by individuals who have a high opinion of the goodness of the Christian God. Instead, many are abandoning their faith or embracing alternative spiritualities because they perceive the God of the Bible as distant, unjust, or even malevolent. This distorted view, as we've discussed, has been influenced by Luciferian thought, radical esoteric feminist constructs, sexual perversion, and globalists with an insatiable lust for power. Yet, it has also been exacerbated by a widespread misunderstanding of Scripture, particularly concerning passages that appear to challenge God's goodness.

This negative perception of God is only deepened when Christians fail to explain or defend these passages or, worse, when they double down on flawed interpretations. Bad theology becomes a poor reflection of God Himself, driving people further from the truth and deeper into the arms of Pagan gods. As Paul rebuked in his letter to the Romans: "The name of God is blasphemed among the Gentiles because of you."[19]

Many well-meaning Christians, in their attempt to offer comfort or explanation, unintentionally misrepresent God's character by making statements like, "God needed another angel in Heaven" in response to a miscarriage, or "God must be trying to teach you something" when someone faces a serious health diagnosis. These phrases, though spoken with good intentions, often push people away from God rather than drawing them closer. They paint a picture of a capricious and distant God, one who flippantly causes senseless suffering or uses tragedy as a lesson at the expense of human pain.

If we are to address these issues and restore confidence in the goodness of God, we must first acknowledge the challenges posed by certain passages in Scripture—verses that have sparked confusion and controversy both inside and outside the church. Let us now examine a few examples of these troubling texts and consider how they should be understood, considering God's true character.

Passages That Challenge Our Understanding of God's Goodness

- Genesis 22: God calls Abraham to sacrifice his son Isaac
- Exodus 9: The hardening of Pharoah's heart
- The Book of Job
- Isaiah 55: "His ways are higher than our ways"
- Matthew 25: The eternal punishment of the wicked
- James 1: "Trials and tribulations"
- John 9: Whether the blind man or his parents were at fault for his blindness
- Hebrews 12: "Disciplining and testing"
- 2 Corinthians 12:7-9: "Paul's thorn in the flesh"

This list is by no means exhaustive, nor could I possibly address every similar passage individually within the pages of this book, even though I would love nothing more than to do so. (For those looking for a more in-depth commentary on individual verses, I addressed many of them in my previous book, *Good God: The One We Want to Believe In But Are Afraid to Embrace.*) The verses I've included serve as examples to illustrate a broader challenge. For those who are new to the Bible, exploring Christianity for the first time, or approaching Scripture with a critical eye, these passages can appear as stumbling blocks. For some, they might even become fodder for a critical spirit, a pretext for rejecting faith outright. For others, even sincere seekers, such verses may create moments of doubt and confusion, clouding their understanding of who God really is.

I want to be clear that my purpose in sharing these examples is not to deepen anyone's doubt or add to the chorus of voices questioning God's goodness. On the contrary, I firmly believe that each of these passages, when properly understood within their biblical context and with a sound theological framework, can be reconciled with the truth of God's good and perfect character—and further demonstrate God's true heart!

For instance, before God "hardened" Pharaoh's heart in Exodus 9, the text shows that Pharaoh first hardened his own heart in defiance of God. God's initial desire was not to destroy Pharaoh, but to "raise you up for this reason, so that I may display My power in you, and that My name may be proclaimed in the whole earth" (Exodus 9:16). Rather than God deciding Pharaoh's fate from the outset, He extended mercy time and again until Pharaoh, through his own stubbornness, left God with no choice but to harden his heart to deliver the Hebrew people. To miss this is to misunderstand God's nature—He is not an erratic destroyer but a merciful Redeemer who gives ample opportunity for repentance before justice is enacted.

A similar issue arises in the opening chapter of James, where some have mistakenly adopted the belief that God is the author of "trials and tribulations." However, verse 13 clarifies, "No one undergoing a trial should say, 'I am being tempted by God,' since God is not tempted by evil, and he himself doesn't tempt anyone."[20] Notably, the same Greek root word for "trials and tribulations" is used throughout the chapter, emphasizing the importance of careful interpretation to avoid drawing false conclusions. Yet, many Christians have ignorantly blamed God for their hardships, a thing the text specifically warns against.

The same can be said of Isaiah 55, quoted earlier, which is commonly used to blindly defend unspeakable horrors with the trite and tired logic that God's "ways are higher than your ways"[21] even though few ever explore the passage deep enough to discern the context of the biblical phrase. One need only murmur the words, and suddenly, all calamities, from train wrecks to tumbling airliners, are rendered inscrutable yet somehow justified—an unfortunate necessity in the cosmic bookkeeping. With thinking like this, is it any wonder that so many struggle to trust the God of the Bible?

For the record, Isaiah 55 doesn't point us toward blind resignation; it calls us to repentance. "Let the wicked one abandon his way and the sinful one his thoughts; let him return to the Lord, so he may have compassion on him, and to our God, for he will freely forgive."[22] Only after this do we hear God declare, "For my thoughts are not your thoughts, and your ways are not my ways."[23] Isaiah 55 doesn't point to God as the causation of human suffering—it magnifies His mercy. His ways are higher not because they are beyond question, but because they are beyond our limited grasp of mercy and grace. The issue, then, is not that God's ways are too high for us—it's that we so often settle for thinking too low of Him.

GOD IS BETTER THAN WE THINK

The task before us, however, is not just to acknowledge these challenges within individual passages, but to equip believers and seekers alike with the tools to confront them. This is the heart of a new apology: providing thoughtful, faithful responses that remove stumbling blocks and affirm the goodness of the God we serve. Ultimately, by grounding ourselves in the big picture of God's goodness, we can approach even the most challenging passages with confidence, knowing that the God who inspired them is perfectly good, just, and trustworthy.

This understanding becomes the filter through which we discern the scriptures, recognizing that any sound biblical interpretation will never portray God as the author of evil or a merciless oppressor of humanity. Instead, it will reveal His justice, mercy, and divine plan to bring redemption to a broken world. And it is through Jesus that we gain clarity on the true character of the Father, as Hebrews 1:3 states, "The Son is the radiance of God's glory and the exact expression of His nature, sustaining all things by His powerful word." The writer of Hebrews reminds us that Jesus is the radiance of God's glory and the lens through which we understand all that God is—His love, His justice, and His goodness. As we look to Christ, we are not left to wrestle with abstract ideas about God but are given the most complete and perfect picture of who He is, bringing light to the shadows of our misunderstandings.

This is particularly important in the context of those who reject or deny God's goodness, especially among neo-Pagans and atheists. Many of them argue that their belief systems are morally superior to the Christian understanding of God. For neo-Pagans, their individual deities or spiritualities are seen as greater, while for atheists, the belief in human autonomy and self-sufficiency is held as morally superior to faith in the Christian God. They often perceive the Christian faith as morally deficient, dismissing God's goodness due to misunderstandings, misinterpretations, or historical debates. Our role, then, is to equip ourselves and others with a biblical framework that demonstrates the consistency of God's goodness and to help those who doubt or reject it see that true moral goodness, justice, and love are found in the Creator, not in the belief systems of man.

One of the clearest and most powerful biblical affirmations of God's character like this is found in 1 John 4:8, which says, "The one who does not love does not know God, because God is love."[24] This simple yet moving statement encapsulates the very heart of God's nature. If God is love, then everything He does, every action He takes, is rooted in His love and, therefore, His goodness. Love is not merely an attribute of God; it is the essence of who He is.

This understanding of God's goodness leads us directly into a vital contrast—how Christianity, unlike Pagan belief systems, provides the only coherent and satisfying foundation for true justice. While the world offers fleeting and flawed versions of justice (often rooted in vengeance or power) the justice of God is perfect, righteous, and redemptive. In Christ, we see justice and mercy fully reconciled, offering the only lasting hope for a broken world and pointing us toward the promise of eternal peace and restoration in Heaven.

THE WAY THINGS OUGHT TO BE

One of my favorite definitions of Heaven is this: "Heaven is where things are how they ought to be." This is not just a statement of future hope, but a declaration of the way things were always meant to be—where divine order is restored and where our longings and desires find their ultimate fulfillment. This is noteworthy when you consider that the desires that drive Pagan culture—the pursuit of women's liberation, the fascination with a collective hive mind, the quest for eternal life, and the yearning for oneness with creation—are in themselves timeless ideas. These longings have been deeply embedded not only in human history but in the human psyche as well.

While I've spent most of this book exposing the dangers that Pagan practices and ideology impose upon society, it's important to recognize that many of the pursuits behind these practices reflect real human desires—desires that ultimately point to our need for something greater than ourselves. But here is where Paganism deteriorates. It may touch on legitimate longings, but it offers no real answers—only counterfeits, distortions, and empty promises that lead people further from the truth rather than toward it.

Christianity does not simply acknowledge these longings; it fulfills them in the only way that is true and lasting. The liberation that Paganism offers is rebellion masquerading as freedom, while Christ offers true freedom through redemption. As Jesus declared, "So if the Son sets you free, you really will be free."[25] But this freedom is not found in the erasure of individuality as Paganism and Marxist ideology suggest. Rather, in Christ, true freedom affirms both our worth and identity, uniting us in a way that preserves, rather than dissolves, who we are. As the Apostle Paul states, "For as the body is one and has many parts, and all the parts of that body, though many, are one body—so also is Christ."[26]

Likewise, the immortality that Paganism chases through reincarnation, medical advancement, or esoteric rituals is nothing more than a drunken illusion, an endless cycle that never truly conquers death. But Christ alone offers the reality of eternal life, declaring, "I am the resurrection and the life. The one who believes in me, even if he dies, will live."[27] And just as only He holds the keys to eternity, only He restores our place within creation—not as worshipers of nature or Gaia, but as stewards under the authority of its Creator. Afterall, "everything was created by him, in heaven and on earth, the visible and the invisible . . . all things have been created through him and for him."[28]

Paganism leads people in circles—forever searching but never finding, always chasing but never arriving. Christ alone is the answer. In Him, every longing finds its fulfillment, every pursuit finds its purpose, and every broken thing is made whole. In Him, things are truly as they ought to be.

Throughout history, Pagan practices have sought to fulfill these deep human longings, but in Christ, we find the true and lasting satisfaction of these desires—where creation, identity, empowerment, and eternity are fully restored in Him.

The following chart explores how Christ fulfills the spiritual longings that Pagan ideologies attempt to address but can never truly satisfy.

Pagan Practice/ Belief	Pagan Description	Biblical Fulfillment in Christ
Gaia Worship	The Earth is a living, divine being, often called "Mother Earth," and should be revered and protected as sacred.	The Earth is not divine, but God's creation, and He alone sustains it. True restoration comes not through worshiping creation or ascribing personhood to the planet, but through Christ who reconciles all things to Himself (Colossians 1:16-17, Romans 8:20-21).
Reincarnation	The soul is reborn into new lives, evolving spiritually until reaching enlightenment or oneness with the universe.	"Just as it is appointed for people to die once—and after this, judgment" (Hebrews 9:27 CSB). Eternal life is not achieved through endless cycles of rebirth but is given as a gift through faith in Christ, who declared, "I am the resurrection and the life" (John 11:25-26, Hebrews 9:27).

Pagan Practice/ Belief	Pagan Description	Biblical Fulfillment in Christ
Sacred Feminine/ Lilith Mythology	Divine power is found in feminine energy, often tied to goddess worship of figures like Lilith, who represents female empowerment and rebellion.	True empowerment comes through Christ, who restores men and women to their God-given identity. In Him, there is no hierarchy of gender value, only spiritual unity and beauty in biological distinctions (Galatians 3:28, 1 Corinthians 11:11-12).
Astrology and Zodiac Signs	The alignment of celestial bodies influences human destiny and personal identity is shaped by astrological signs.	Our identity and future are not shaped by the stars, but by the One who created them. While we are called to exercise personal agency and responsibility, it is Christ, the Light of the world, who gives us true direction and purpose. He, as our Creator, directs our steps, guiding us in ways far superior to mere celestial bodies (Psalm 139:16, John 8:12).

Pagan Practice/ Belief	Pagan Description	Biblical Fulfillment in Christ
Pantheism/ Oneness with Nature/ Oneness with the Universe	Everything is divine, and the goal is to merge with or realize one's unity with the universe.	God is not an impersonal force, but a personal Creator who invites us into an intimate relationship with Him through Christ (John 17:3, Colossians 1:16-17).
Witchcraft and Manifestation	Through spells, rituals, or the law of attraction, individuals can manipulate energy or summon spiritual forces to achieve desires.	True power and provision come from Christ, who calls us to seek first His kingdom, trusting that He will provide all we need (Matthew 6:33, Ephesians 3:20).
Chakra/ Energy Centers	Awakening a coiled serpent energy at the base of the spine leads to spiritual enlightenment and divine power.	True spiritual renewal comes through the Holy Spirit, not hidden energies. In Christ, we receive the power of God, not through self-exaltation, but through surrender (John 14:26, 2 Timothy 1:7).

Pagan Practice/ Belief	Pagan Description	Biblical Fulfillment in Christ
Hive Mind/ Collective Consciousness	The desire for a unified collective consciousness, where individuality dissolves into a shared identity or purpose.	True unity is found in Christ, where the body of believers is united, yet individual, each member having distinct gifts and purpose within the whole. In Christ, personal worth is affirmed, and the body of believers functions as one (1 Corinthians 12:12-13).
One World Order/Global Theosophy	The pursuit of global unity and control, often seeking to erase national, ethnic, or ideological distinctions in favor of a singular global government or worldview.	God's kingdom is not of this world, and Christ is the true ruler who will establish His reign over all creation, but His kingdom is not built on human systems or forced unity. The ultimate fulfillment is in Christ's return, where every tribe, tongue, and nation will worship Him (Revelation 21:1-4, Philippians 2:9-11).

TWO TYPES OF FREEDOM

Ultimately, what Pagan practices and philosophies offer are incomplete, fleeting answers to the deepest human longings: the desire for liberation, identity, empowerment, and eternity. They promise freedom, but it's a freedom built on illusions, where fulfillment is always just out of reach, and the cycle of desire and disillusionment continues. Christianity, however, speaks to those same longings, cutting through Pagan mysticism and darkness, to clearly reveal our truest desires. Through His grace, what was broken by sin and the deception of the devil is restored, and we are made whole. It is in Christ that the eternal satisfaction our hearts ache for is found: where justice is perfectly embodied, creation is restored to its rightful place, our identity is firmly rooted, our true freedom is realized, and our longing for eternity is culminated in His endless grace. The Gospel of Jesus Christ holds the promise that every desire, every pursuit, and every yearning finds its perfect fulfillment in Him—now and forever more.

Now, contrast this with the Pagan vision of freedom—a vision that insists the highest form of liberation lies in the ability to become one's own god. It's a seductive lie that promises the power to transcend all external authority and shape one's own destiny, unchecked by moral boundaries. From ancient Greek philosophy to modern-day New Age ideologies, Paganism has always told us that true freedom is found in the rejection of limits, the pursuit of bodily autonomy, and the desire to be self-sufficient—gods of our own universe. This is the freedom of self-exaltation: the belief that liberation comes when we cast off all external restraints, making ourselves the ultimate authority over our lives.

But the irony is this: the more one strives to become like God on their own terms, the further one drifts from the true God. As such, the freedom promised by Paganism—freedom without moral absolutes—ultimately becomes a form of enslavement. It was this sort of enslavement that Paul warned the Colossian church about: "Be careful that no one takes you captive through philosophy and empty deceit based on human tradition, based on the elements of the world, rather than Christ."[29] Enslavement to the whims of passion, ambition, and endless striving leads us further from our true identity. Paul understood that the more we seek to define ourselves apart from God, the more we lose sight of who we truly are. Paul's friend and counterpart, the Apostle Peter, provided a similar admonition, calling such beliefs "destructive heresies"[30] based upon "made-up stories"[31] from false teachers who "promise them freedom, but they themselves are slaves of corruption."[32] Both Paul and Peter remind us that the road apart from God is a path that leads to spiritual emptiness, a perpetual chase for self-actualization that never truly satisfies.

The apostles' warnings, though, don't just pinpoint an individual danger, but a societal one as well. When freedom is untethered from moral truth, it can easily devolve into chaos. This is where Paganism, with its rejection of moral absolutes, becomes a real threat to any nation, especially America. The Founders understood that true freedom could not exist without a moral foundation. A society built on unchecked liberty (like the Pagan visions of freedom) would fall prey to the same forces of greed and godless passions Paul and Peter warned against. The Founders recognized that true freedom (the kind that could sustain a just and thriving society) was only possible when tethered to a moral framework that acknowledged the boundaries of human will and the need for God's guidance. Said another way, they understood that human independence is only truly realized through divine dependence. Capturing this sentiment perfectly in a letter to the Massachusetts Militia in 1798, John Adams warned of the dangers that would come if Americans were to stray from Christian virtue. He wrote:

> Because we have no government armed with power capable
> of contending with human passions unbridled by morality
> and religion. Avarice, ambition, revenge, or gallantry would

*break the strongest cords of our Constitution as a whale
goes through a net. Our Constitution was made only for a
moral and religious people. It is wholly inadequate to the
government of any other.*[33]

For Adams, liberty wasn't just about freedom from oppression—it was about the freedom to live virtuously, to live in harmony with the moral order that Christianity provided. The Founders knew that the Constitution, though a brilliant political document, could only thrive in a society where the people, at their core, were committed to justice, responsibility, and godly virtue. And that virtue, in their view, was best nurtured within the context of Christian faith.

But today, as Pagan ideologies rise to prominence in modern culture, we see how this ideal of freedom is under siege. The falsity of freedom as absolute autonomy—freedom without restraint, freedom that disregards moral and spiritual boundaries, freedom that cannot discern between genders or acknowledge the wickedness of slaughtering the unborn—is increasingly pervasive. This resurgence of self-sufficiency and self-exaltation undercuts the very spirit of freedom that America is built upon. As more people embrace this distorted view of liberty, we will continue to witness a nation's understanding of freedom unraveling as it becomes increasingly removed from the moral framework that once sustained it.

The truth is that Christianity offers a radically different kind of freedom—one that is not about ascension through our own strength, but about surrender. It doesn't call us to climb up to become gods, but to lay down our self-sufficiency and receive grace. The Gospel doesn't promise that we will become our own gods; it promises that we will become like God—a far richer, deeper, and more liberating reality.

As the apostle Paul writes, "For those he foreknew he also predestined to be conformed to the image of his Son, so that he would be the firstborn among many brothers and sisters."[34] This is the true promise of freedom—to be conformed to the image of Christ. Not through our own effort, but through grace. And in receiving that grace, we become who we were always meant to be. The image of God, which in Paganism is a goal to be seized, in Christianity is a gift to be received—and it is in receiving this gift that we find our true identity, our true freedom.

A NEW APOLOGY FOR A LOST WORLD

While what I have provided above is little more than a humble inception to the new apology that must be crafted to counter the encroaching Paganism in America, I pray it will inspire a new generation of Justin Martyrs and Athanasiuses to rise up and boldly proclaim the faith. Will this be enough to convince all who are lost? I suspect not. However, it is my earnest hope that those caught in the deception of Pagan practices—those who are truly searching for divine truth and spiritual revelation—will see past the noise of this world and recognize the truth that Paul proclaimed in Athens.

In his address to the Athenians, Paul didn't simply criticize their false worship; he boldly proclaimed the truth of the living God, the Creator of all. He offered not just an intellectual argument, but an invitation to salvation—a call to repent and turn from ignorance to the true knowledge of God. As Paul said in the middle of Areopagus:

> People of Athens, I see that you are extremely religious in
> every respect. For as I was passing through and observing the

objects of your worship, I even found an altar on which was
inscribed: TO AN UNKNOWN GOD. Therefore, what you
worship in ignorance, this I proclaim to you. The God who
made the world and everything in it, He is Lord of heaven
and earth and does not live in shrines made by hands.
Neither is He served by human hands, as though He needed
anything, since He Himself gives everyone life and breath and
all things. From one man He has made every nationality to
live over the whole earth and has determined their appointed
times and the boundaries of where they live. He did this so
that they might seek God, and perhaps they might reach out
and find Him, though He is not far from each one of us. For
in Him we live and move and have our being, as even some
of your own poets have said, "For we are also His offspring."
Since we are God's offspring, then, we shouldn't think that
the divine nature is like gold or silver or stone, an image
fashioned by human art and imagination. Therefore, having
overlooked the times of ignorance, God now commands all
people everywhere to repent, because He has set a day when
He is going to judge the world in righteousness by the man
He has appointed. He has provided proof of this to everyone
by raising Him from the dead.[35]

This is the message we are called to bring to our culture—a culture steeped in idols of all kinds, seeking answers in everything but the Creator. As believers, we must speak the truth with boldness, not simply pointing out the errors of Paganism, but proclaiming the hope of the Gospel: the God who created the heavens and the earth has made a way for us to know Him through Christ, and He commands all to repent. Lest we forget, the day of judgment is coming, and we are called to live in light of that reality.

But against the powers of darkness, proclamation alone is not enough. As the body of Christ, we must not only speak the truth—we must also demonstrate it. Jesus said, "You will receive power when the Holy Spirit has come on you, and you will be my witnesses."[36] The power of the Holy Spirit enables us to live in a way that reflects God's kingdom here and now. Without the Spirit, our words are empty; with the Spirit, our lives become a living testimony to the truth of God's love and power. As Paul reminded the Corinthians, "For our Gospel did not come to you in word only, but also in power, in the Holy Spirit, and with full assurance."[37] As the world increasingly turns to the signs and wonders of witchcraft and Pagan practices, Christians must stand firm, empowered by the Spirit, to demonstrate the greater power of Christ.

We cannot accomplish this mission alone. The task before us is too great for individual efforts. It requires the collective strength of the church, unified in purpose and empowered by the Holy Spirit, to be the hands and feet of Christ in a world that desperately needs Him. As we look ahead, we must embrace our role as the church—not just as a place of worship, but as the living, breathing witness of God's redemptive work in the world. It is through the church, the body of Christ, that God intends to bring transformation. The future of that transformation lies in the church of tomorrow—a church that is ready to rise, rooted in Christ and empowered by the Spirit, to meet the challenges of a world that needs the light of the Gospel more than ever.

NINE

THE CHURCH
OF TOMORROW

OVERCOMING COMPLACENCY

A popular chain bookstore in my hometown has three large sections devoted to witchcraft and Pagan reading materials. The shelves are filled with titles such as *The World's Most Haunted Places, Herbal Magick, Ancestral Magic,* and *The Path to Becoming a Witch.* There is nothing unique about my city, though. Shelves like these are found across the country, and if anything, my state, embedded with Midwest conservative values, is less saturated with this material—making the situation even more frightening.

What's most striking to me, however, is that despite the significant rise in Pagan revivalism and witchcraft, I can't think of a single church—except for my own—that has done any meaningful teaching to address this Pagan uprising. Sure, some churches have tackled cultural issues, and the bolder ones (especially leading up to the 2024 election) have taken a stand on political matters, but few seem to grasp the full extent of the threat against orthodox Christianity that is quietly gaining ground.

I think this partially stems from the fact that the median age of clergy in America is steadily increasing, from age "50 in 2000 to 57 in 2020,"[1] creating a wider generational divide between ministers and the young people they desperately need to reach. As a result, many of the physical and digital gathering places for both

Gen Alpha and Gen Z where spiritual conversations are happening (school lunchrooms and TikTok livestreams) are inaccessible to pastors, leaving them unaware of the cultural shifts and spiritual battles unfolding in these spaces.

Please hear me though—I'm not saying that every pastor needs to start dressing in the latest fashion trend from the TikTok shop and mastering Gen Z lingo, like "bet," "skibidi toilet," and "sigma" to fit in, but pastors should be looking for ways to stay relevant and to understand the times. Unfortunately, the church has been classically late to the party on many all-too-important conversations. How many churches were silent regarding *Roe v. Wade*? How many ignored gay marriage, hoping it would just go away? How many remained quiet during the 2024 election campaign for fear of dividing their congregations, despite clear demonic policies being presented by one party?

For example, in Arizona, a 2024 ballot initiative called Proposition 139 introduced radical expansions in abortion access, deeply undermining the sanctity of life in the desert state. Sadly though, some of the largest churches in the state were silent on the issue, which likely led to its passing. Condemning their inaction, Turning Point USA founder Charlie Kirk said, "They're completely silent on the most radical abortion measure in the country. . . . Totally silent."[2]

At times, I think the hesitation to get involved stems from fear—fear of losing members, fear of jeopardizing their church's 501(c)(3) status, or fear of public pushback. But with issues like abortion, Critical Race Theory, and the rising interest in witchcraft and Pagan ideology, my fear is that the silence is not just about these external fears. It's because pastors aren't willing to learn new things or sharpen their skills to address, head-on, the spiritual needs of their communities. I fear this is nothing more than spiritual laziness. As Proverbs 24:30-34 (CSB) warns:

I went past the field of a sluggard, past the vineyard of
someone who has no sense; thorns had come up everywhere,
the ground was covered with weeds, and the stone wall was
in ruins. I applied my heart to what I observed and learned a
lesson from what I saw: A little sleep, a little slumber, a little
folding of the hands to rest—and poverty will come on you
like a thief and scarcity like an armed man.

As much as I don't want to admit it, spiritual complacency may very well be the defining characteristic of the modern church. As the head of TPUSA Faith working alongside Charlie Kirk, I had a front-row seat to the 2024 election. During this time, I saw countless pastors—many of whom I know personally—who were simply unwilling to address the cultural issues facing our nation, not to mention the state of Arizona. Like the servant in the Parable of the Talents,[3] they were spiritual sluggards who refused to invest what the Master entrusted to them. And as a result, they did nothing.

Just like the neglected vineyard in Proverbs, the consequences of the church's inaction are becoming increasingly apparent. And without a significant wake-up call, I fear the church is in danger of burying its collective head in the sand while the Christian faith is steadily deconstructed around it. As I say often, although God wins in the end at the Second Coming, it doesn't mean the church in America will always thrive. We see ancient European cathedrals that serve as beautiful reminders of a place where Christianity once thrived but is now all but empty. America, if we're not careful, could share the same fate—though, unlike Europe's grand cathedrals, our modern, mostly unremarkable, church buildings probably won't become tourist attractions anytime soon.

To avoid this, we must face the facts. The theological walls that once stood strong are beginning to crumble and weeds of compromise and confusion are taking root. This is no time for hesitation or fear. Spiritual laziness is a luxury we cannot afford in the face of a crumbling world. The call to action is unmistakable and cannot be ignored: The church must rise with boldness and engage in the fight for truth now before it's too late.

MISSION AHEAD

Like any battle, victory won't come from focusing on a single front. Success will require the church to strengthen its position across a variety of critical areas—many of which have been neglected for far too long. Key priorities include:

- Deepen discipleship rooted in primary Christian doctrine
- Develop a roadmap for Christian engagement in politics and the public square
- Leverage technology for the advancement of the Gospel
- Redouble efforts to reach today's youth
- Implement a practical strategy for evangelism
- Directly combat false doctrines and Pagan ideologies
- Renew interest in spiritual gifts

Each of these areas represents a vital front in the spiritual battle to defeat the Pagan uprising and to win back the heart of America for Christ. Neglecting even one area could leave the church vulnerable to cultural erosion or diminished Kingdom returns. As such, I've devoted a good portion of the remainder of this book to understanding each of these areas fully and to creating a stratagem for the Church of Tomorrow to employ to successfully confront the Pagan agenda.

Before we move forward, though, it's worth defining what we mean by "the Church of Tomorrow." It sounds spiritually romantic to envision a unified Christian movement—one mind, one voice, lifting high the banner of Christ, boldly proclaiming the Gospel and fearlessly pushing back the darkness. While this is a worthy ideal, history tells a different story.

Instead, we find a fragmented body comprising hundreds of denominations, each with its own doctrines, dogmas, and debates—everything from eternal security to modesty standards—all while claiming a corner on the truth. This theological diversity makes the pursuit of unity seem daunting, if not impossible, often requiring endless debate that few have the patience or courage to endure. But true Christian unity does not come from theological minimalism or superficial ecumenism. It comes from a shared commitment to the core truths of Scripture—the very truths that once united believers across generations. If we can recover and re-establish these foundational truths, then we, as the Church of Tomorrow, can answer Paul's call to "keep the unity of the Spirit through the bond of peace,"[4] standing firm as one body grounded in truth. Unfortunately, this is more easily said than done.

THE WHOLE TRUTH

"It seems obvious to most believers that there is a solemn pastoral duty to teach and defend correct Christian doctrine,"[5] wrote Thomas C. Oden, a twentieth-century American theologian and author of *After Modernity—What?* Yet, as Oden observed, although the "unifying center of the [Christian] tradition"[6] should be clear, it often isn't. Diagnosing a problem that remains strikingly relevant today, he explained:

> *The problem is that this pastoral duty has not been vigorously pursued. The unifying center has not been*

sufficiently defined. The ancient heresies flourish in every
quarter unrecognized as such, often baptized and blessed by
the parson's affable smile. After all, who needs controversy;
and don't forget, the membership rolls could easily suffer
from such probing questions.[7]

Oden's warning grows more urgent with time: The need to return to a clearly defined, primary Christian doctrine is essential for preserving unity and truth in an age of theological compromise and Pagan revival. In the early centuries of the church, this was achieved through prayerful councils and carefully constructed creeds—those forged in the fires of fierce theological battles. Men like Athanasius or Basil of Caesarea defended truth with unwavering courage, often paying a heavy personal cost to preserve sound doctrine for future generations.

Among these creeds, the Apostles' Creed stands as a vital, unifying declaration of Christian faith. G.K. Chesterton said it summarized "the central Christian theology" and stood synonymous with "orthodoxy."[8] Though not exhaustive in its scope, it offers a foundational summary of biblical truth that uniquely guards against heresy and anchors believers to the essentials of the Gospel. Developed as early as the second century,[9] the creed reads as follows:[10]

I believe in God, the Father Almighty,
Creator of heaven and earth,

And in Jesus Christ, His only Son, our Lord,
Who was conceived by the Holy Spirit,
Born of the Virgin Mary,
Suffered under Pontius Pilate,
Was crucified, died, and was buried;
He descended to the dead.

On the third day, He rose again from the dead;
He ascended into heaven,
And is seated at the right hand of God, the Father Almighty;
From there, He will come to judge the living and the dead.

I believe in the Holy Spirit,
The holy catholic Church,
The communion of saints,
The forgiveness of sins,
The resurrection of the body,
And the life everlasting.

Amen.

More than just a beautiful mantra or even a unifying dogma, The Apostles' Creed provides a fortified wall of truth against heresies and false doctrines of all kinds, including the creeping influence of Pagan revivalism and Woke ideology. St. Augustine explained that "underneath these few words"[11] of the Creed are the foundational truths of the Christian faith and that there exists robust protection "against the insidious assaults of the heretics."[12] By affirming these core doctrines of the Christian faith, believers are anchored in timeless truths that transcend cultural trends, equipping the church to stand firm in an age of confusion and compromise. Each line serves as a clear and uncompromising declaration of orthodoxy preserving the faith "once for all delivered to the saints" (Jude 1:3).

"I believe in God, the Father Almighty, Creator of heaven
and earth."

In contrast to Pagan beliefs, evolutionary scientists, and New Age globalists, this first line affirms that God is the supreme Creator of all things, both seen and unseen. It declares the foundational truth of a personal, powerful God who exists out-side of time and space, initiating and sustaining all of creation. While some Pagan practices, like those invoking Gaia or other nature-centered deities, might claim the universe is the product of a divine mother or an impersonal, self-organizing force, the Creed makes a bold statement against this. It emphasizes that God is not a distant, abstract force or an impersonal energy but the intentional, sovereign Father who created the heavens and the Earth with purpose and design. This rejects the pantheistic view that the divine is synonymous with the Earth or nature itself, reaf-firming that the Creator stands above and beyond His creation, shaping the universe according to His will.

Additionally, this line affirms God's establishment of the order of the universe, which includes His design for male and female, marriage, and gender. It speaks to the current cultural confusion over gender and sexuality by reaffirming that God's creation is purposeful and reflects a divine order. The concept of marriage as between one man and one woman is embedded in this creation narrative, showing that the roles of men and women are part of a larger, God-ordained structure. Furthermore, the Creed reminds us that God is the author of life, giving value to human life from the womb to the tomb, as designed and initiated by Him. This counters modern views that devalue human life or distort the sanctity of life, reaffirming that every human being is created in the image of God and is precious in His sight, regardless of age, circumstance, or stage of life.

"And in Jesus Christ, His only Son, our Lord."

More than a teacher or a prophet, this line proclaims that Jesus is the only Son of God, the Christ, our Lord. In an era of Woke pluralism, which often diminishes the divinity of Jesus, this statement reminds us that salvation is found in Christ alone, dismantling work-based theology and self-righteousness. It also directly challenges the syncretistic idea that all paths lead to God, affirming that Christ's sacrificial work is the only means of salvation. By grounding salvation in Christ alone, the Creed destroys ideologies that seek to elevate human effort, spiritual enlightenment, or collective identity as the source of redemption.

"Who was conceived by the Holy Spirit, born of the Virgin Mary."

This line affirms the supernatural nature of Jesus' conception and birth, emphasizing the miraculous incarnation. More than just a metaphor, it underscores that Jesus entered history divinely and supernaturally, bypassing sinful human nature. It challenges ideologies that attempt to downplay the significance of divine intervention in the world, asserting that Jesus' birth was not only a historical event but also a divine act of grace. This contradicts the notion that Jesus was merely an enlightened man who ascended to the divine. Instead, it affirms that Jesus entered the world through a divine incarnation with His very existence being supernatural from beginning to end.

"Suffered under Pontius Pilate, was crucified, died, and was buried."

By mentioning Pilate, this line of the Creed grounds Jesus' suffering in historical reality, confronting any belief that downplays the gravity of Christ's sacrifice. Unlike Pagan practices rooted in meaningless mythologies, the Gospel of Jesus is fixed within a concrete historical event supported by substantial evidence affirming its authenticity. The crucifixion, death, and burial of Jesus are central to Christianity's message of atonement. This challenges ideologies that minimize sin, such as Woke language that often downplays the need for personal redemption, insisting that Christ's death was essential to atone for humanity's sins. On a personal level, reflecting on Christ's suffering forces us to confront the painful truth that it is our sin that placed Him on the Cross. Yet, it is His immeasurable love for us that not only held Him there but also transformed His sacrifice into the ultimate act of grace and redemption. This revelation exposes the fallacy of redefining morality based on subjective views, reminding us that true redemption begins with recognizing our faults and embracing the necessity of Christ's sacrificial love.

"He descended to the dead."

In the face of modern ideologies that deny, distort, or even glorify the concept of Hell, this phrase upholds the truth of Christ's victory over death and the grave. This statement affirms that Jesus fully experienced the depths of human suffering and death, even descending to the place of the dead,* to conquer sin and death completely. It challenges any belief that avoids confronting the ultimate reality of human suffering and eternal separation from God.

"On the third day, He rose again from the dead."

This line underscores the centrality of the resurrection and is the cornerstone of the Christian faith. This truth strikes against

---

* The phrase "descended to Hell" in the Apostles' Creed has been the subject of theological debate, particularly concerning whether it refers to "Hell" or "Sheol." Traditionally, "Hell" in this context has been understood as the place of the dead or the realm of the damned. However, some scholars argue that the original text likely referred to "Sheol," a Hebrew term for the underworld or the place of the dead, which in early Jewish thought was not necessarily a place of punishment but a shadowy existence where all souls went, regardless of their righteousness. The shift from "Sheol" to "Hell" reflects a later Christian understanding of Christ's descent as involving a confrontation with the forces of evil and death. This phrase, regardless of its specific interpretation, emphasizes Christ's solidarity with the dead and His triumph over death itself, signifying His complete participation in the human experience of suffering and death.

ideologies that dismiss the bodily resurrection or eternal life, such as the materialistic worldview of secularism or certain Eastern-influenced Pagan practices that deny the eternal individuality of the soul. The resurrection affirms that Christ's victory over death is the foundation of our hope, empowering us to overcome sin and live in the light of His resurrection. Writing of this hope, the Apostle Peter declared, "Blessed be the God and Father of our Lord Jesus Christ. Because of His great mercy, He has given us new birth into a living hope through the resurrection of Jesus Christ from the dead."[13]

"He ascended into heaven, and is seated at the right hand of God, the Father Almighty."

Here, the Creed emphasizes Christ's divine authority directly from the Father, through which He reigns supreme from Heaven. It challenges ideologies that reduce Christ to a mere historical figure, a powerless symbol, or just one other god in a Pagan pantheon. By asserting that Jesus is seated at the right hand of God, it emphasizes His ongoing Lordship over all creation, offering a stark contrast to the often horizontal, politically driven ideologies of the modern world, including those that seek to build utopias through human effort.

"From there, He will come to judge the living and the dead."

This line reinforces the truth that Christ's return will bring ultimate justice. In a world where secular justice systems and Woke ideologies often fail to deliver true justice, the return of Christ as the final judge assures that all wrongs will be righted according to God's perfect standard. It challenges the growing trend of relativism and moral ambiguity, affirming that absolute truth and accountability are foundational to the Christian faith.

"I believe in the Holy Spirit."

In an age marked by spiritual confusion and mysticism, where New Age ideologies often blur the lines between the divine and the self, this line affirms that the Holy Spirit is not a mere force, vibe, or mystical power but a distinct Person within the Godhead. This phrase of the Apostles' Creed safeguards us against heresy by declaring that the Holy Spirit, as the Third Person of the Trinity, is to be revered and acknowledged for His unique and personal role. It emphasizes that the Spirit's work is to glorify Christ and empower believers to live following God's will and stands in opposition to modern ideas of self-deification and spiritual relativism that reduce the Holy Spirit to an impersonal, unknowable force. Not only that, but the indwelling presence of the Holy Spirit also affirms our adoption as sons and daughters of God, as 1 John testifies: "This is how we know that we remain in Him and He in us: He has given us of His Spirit."[14]

"The holy catholic Church."

This line underscores the universal* and unified nature of the church, rejecting division and fragmentation. In a time of deep denominational divides and conflicting ideologies, including within the church, this statement calls the body of Christ to unity. It affirms that the church, while diverse in expression, is united in

---

* In the context of the Apostles' Creed, the phrase "the holy catholic church" refers to the universal body of believers, not to any specific denomination or to the Roman Catholic Church. The term "catholic" comes from the Greek word *katholikos*, meaning "universal" or "whole." Protestants affirm that the church is universal in scope, encompassing all believers in Christ across time and space, regardless of denominational affiliation. The word "holy" indicates that the church, though made up of imperfect people, is set apart for God's purposes, consecrated by the work of Christ and the indwelling of the Holy Spirit. For Protestants, this line underscores the belief that the church is not defined by human structures but by the presence of true believers who hold to the Gospel of Jesus Christ.

primary doctrine and mission, challenging the divisive and often agenda-driven nature of modern Christian discourse. Of all the statements of the Creed, this may be the most divisive, as some will see this as elevating only their denomination to the exclusion of all others. We must resist this temptation, though, to promote an elitist Christian denominationalism. Unity across denominational lines remains necessary if we are to confront the Pagan uprising, and this is only possible with denominational humility, by receiving those who hold to secondary and tertiary differences from ourselves with grace while standing unified against those who make a mockery of the faith by departing from the primary truths of God's Word.

"The communion of saints."

This truth affirms the unity of believers across time and space, showing that the church is a living body that transcends individualism, fragmentation, and the self-centered ideologies of a neo-Pagan world. In contrast to the modern iterations of Woke religious practices discussed in this book, which promote division through identity politics and personal grievances, the communion of saints unites us with Christians throughout history, past and future, bound by a shared faith in Christ. Our communion is not rooted in shared victimhood or personal agendas but in His sacrifice on the cross. In this, we remember that true unity is found in His suffering, not our own, as we are drawn together by His redemption, rather than unity in some form of Marx-inspired mutual struggle.

"The forgiveness of sins."

This line affirms the essential doctrine of grace, declaring that forgiveness is a gift from God, not something earned by human effort or activism. It directly confronts Pagan practices and Woke ideologies that often focus on personal responsibility, guilt, or social justice as the means of atonement, instead pointing to the completed work of Christ on the cross as the only means by which sins are forgiven and redemption is granted. This truth forces us to face the reality of sin, reminding us of those certain behaviors—such as sexual immorality and the normalization of depravity—that are not merely differences of opinion but transgressions against God's holiness. The forgiveness of sins calls us to repentance, not to redefine or normalize sin, challenging us to align our lives with God's standards rather than the ever-shifting moral landscape of modern culture.

"The resurrection of the body."

This statement reaffirms the hope of physical resurrection and eternal life, directly confronting neo-Pagan practices that often elevate the spirit while disregarding the sanctity of the body. It challenges the materialistic worldview that sees the body as disposable or irrelevant and counters modern ideologies that treat human beings as mere physical matter or reduce bodily existence to transient pleasure or self-worship. The Christian belief in the resurrection upholds the body as sacred, emphasizing that our physical form is integral to God's redemptive plan. This truth affirms that the body is not to be abandoned or idolized, but rather, it will be transformed and glorified in the eternal life promised by Christ.

"And the life everlasting."

This line affirms the eternal nature of Christian hope, sharply contrasting the fleeting utopias and transient globalist agendas that many modern neo-Pagan ideologies promote, which often elevate earthly power, progressive control, or personal fulfillment as ultimate goals. It challenges the obsession with immediate gratification, short-term political gains, and worldly progressiv-ism, redirecting our focus to the eternal promise of life with God. In a world consumed by self-worship, temporary solutions, and the pursuit of fleeting pleasures, this statement calls believers to anchor their lives in the unshakeable hope of everlasting life, urg-ing them to live with an eternal perspective that transcends the illusions and distractions of this world.

MOVING FORWARD

Now that we have considered the dangers of spiritual com-placency and the importance of finding our unity in primary Christian truths, it's time to focus on practical steps believers can take to equip themselves for the battle against the rising tide of Paganism and cultural confusion. After all, simply knowing the truth is not enough. As author Francis A. Schaeffer reminds us in his classic work, *How Should We Then Live?* we must live it out:

> As Christians, we are not only to know the right worldview, the worldview that tells us the truth of what is but consciously to act upon that worldview so as to influence society in all its parts and facets across the whole spectrum of life, as much as we can to the extent of our individual and collective ability.[15]

To embrace Schaeffer's advice and effectively confront the challenges before us—ensuring that we do not repeat the mis-takes of the past—the church must focus its efforts on the key areas we've already discussed. After all, we need a church not only deeply rooted in its faith but also actively engaged in the world around it.

In the following section, we will revisit these essential strategies for strengthening discipleship, engaging the culture, and advancing the Gospel in today's rapidly shifting landscape, aiming to create a clear and decisive roadmap for resisting the expanding influence of Paganism. These strategies will be crucial to ensure that we rise to the occasion, remain steadfast in the truth, and make a tangible difference for the Kingdom of God.

THE FINAL BATTLE PLAN

As we stand on the precipice of this cultural shift, what author Eric Metaxas refers to as America's "third existential crisis,"[16] the time has come to put into action a comprehensive, decisive strategy that not only defends the truth but also brings light into the darkness of the growing totalitarian Pagan uprising. To accomplish this, we must focus on the essential steps needed to combat the rise of Paganism so we can fortify believers' faith, strategically spread the Gospel, and reclaim the public square for God's glory.

1. Deepen Discipleship Rooted in Primary Christian Doctrine

The first and most crucial step in our battle plan is to deepen discipleship by developing a widespread commitment to primary doctrine. While it may seem like we already addressed this in the above summary of the Apostles' Creed, this is only a starting point. The church must help its members contextualize the foundations of the faith into relevant doctrines regarding today's toughest issues. Carl Trueman writes more deeply on this:

*The church's teaching on gender, marriage, and sex is a
function of her teaching on what it means to be human. The
doctrines of creation, fall, redemption, and consummation
are important foundations for addressing the specific
challenges of our time. . . . In short, we can stand strong at
this cultural moment and address the specific challenges we
face only if our foundations in God's truth are broad and
deep. This means that the chaotic nature of our times is
no excuse for abandoning the church's task of teaching her
people the whole counsel of God.*[17]

As Trueman states, chaotic times are not a sufficient reason
to abandon truth. If anything, they should compel us even more
to proclaim it. After all, without a deep and unwavering commitment to the truth of the Word, believers will be vulnerable to false
ideologies. To take action to prevent this, we should:

- *Develop Robust Teaching.* Churches must prioritize
  sound theological education at every level—Sunday
  schools, Bible studies, seminars, sermons, and books.
  Discipleship must move beyond surface-level Christianity
  into a profound, lifelong commitment to understanding
  the Scriptures, the character of God, and the essential
  doctrines of our faith.
- *Study Church History.* Church history provides valuable
  lessons on how to navigate false doctrines and Pagan
  ideologies that have threatened the faith throughout the
  centuries. By studying how the early Church responded
  to heresies and cultural pressures, we can gain insight into
  how to confront similar challenges today. Learning from
  both the triumphs and failures of those who came before
  us, we can better stand firm against the rising tide of false

beliefs and Paganism, ensuring that we remain grounded in the truth of Scripture.

- *Contextualize the Truth.* As Christians, we are called to apply timeless biblical truths to the issues of our day, not retreat into a corner and hope the world changes on its own. We must equip our churches to understand how the core doctrines of Christianity shape and influence our view of pivotal social issues like marriage, family, gender, religious liberty, and government. A biblical worldview is not just a personal guide to salvation; it is the lens through which we must view the world around us. We cannot afford to remain silent or disengaged on matters such as the radicalization of gender ideology, the push for abortion on demand, or the encroaching influence of globalist policies.

2. Develop a Roadmap for Christian Engagement in Politics and the Public Square

The battle for cultural dominance is not fought in church buildings alone. It extends into the public square, the halls of government, and the arenas where ideas compete for dominance. Christian engagement in politics is not optional—it is critical if we are to reclaim this land for Christ and resist the relentless tide of ideologies that seek to obliterate biblical truth. Consider this timeless warning from author Francis A. Schaeffer:

> If we as Christians do not speak out as authoritarian governments grow from within or come from outside, eventually we or our children will be the enemy of society and the state. No truly authoritarian government can tolerate those who have a real absolute by which to judge its

arbitrary absolutes, and who speak out and act upon that
absolute.[18]

Yet, despite having this "real absolute," far too many Christians still refuse to enter the fray, content to stand on the sidelines while the very soul of our nation is at stake. Such complacent and cowardly behavior must be called out and corrected. Here are three ideas for getting started:

- *Engage in Public Discourse.* Christians must step beyond the church walls and actively engage in shaping the cultural and political landscape. This isn't about aligning with one political party—it's about championing biblical principles in every aspect of society. From policy to education to social issues, Christians must make our voices heard, advocating for truth, justice, and morality in every discussion. The fight over life, marriage, and religious freedom is a moral battle and we can no longer afford to stay silent. Thankfully, there are many practical ways to get involved: present at school board meetings on key issues, write an op-ed for a local or national news outlet, or speak out on social media about moral and civil issues that reflect a biblical worldview. These actions allow us to be active participants in the conversations shaping our society, standing firm on the unchanging truth of God's Word.
- *Support Faithful Leadership.* Our nation needs godly men and women in positions of authority, not for personal gain, but to be stewards of God's truth in public service. We must prioritize supporting leaders who will stand strong against the forces of Paganism, secularism, and moral decline. We need to encourage Christian

involvement in politics—not as a means of gaining power, but as a means of bringing God's truth into the public arena. The rise of godless leadership threatens everything we hold dear, and it's time to ensure those who align with biblical values are equipped to lead. (*TPUSA Faith has a variety of free resources to assist in this area, including Rick Green's Biblical Citizenship course. Find out more at tpusafaith.com.*)

- **Advocate for True Biblical Justice.** This is a fight for the soul of our nation, and Christians must not remain passive. As we "occupy until He comes,"[19] we must advocate for policies rooted in biblical justice, defend the unborn, protect children against radical indoctrination, and uphold the sanctity of marriage and family. From the statehouse to the schoolhouse, we must demand that the laws and policies reflect God's truth, not the subjective morals of a secular culture. This is more than just political activism; it is a moral imperative that will shape the future of our families, communities, and nation.

3. Leverage Technology for the Advancement of the Gospel

As it has been said, "He who controls the media, controls the mind," and unfortunately, the forces of Paganism and secularism have long dominated the media landscape, shaping narratives that distort truth and undermine traditional values. In today's digital age, where social media platforms, streaming services, and news outlets wield unprecedented power, Christians cannot afford to sit idly by. We must actively engage with these platforms, not merely as consumers, but as creators of content that upholds biblical truths. By reclaiming the digital space we not only evangelize but equip believers with the tools to discern the shifting tides of modern culture, turning the very mediums that seek to deceive into instruments of truth and transformation. Here are some ways in which Christians can actively stay relevant in our approach:

- *Create Gospel-Centered Content.* The internet is flooded with harmful content that shapes the hearts and minds of millions. Christians must flood the digital space with viral-ready content that is Gospel-centered, doctrinally sound, and designed to engage the next generation. From podcasts to YouTube channels and social media platforms, we must make it a point to proclaim the truth of the Gospel everywhere people are gathering online. Suggestions include: short-form videos of street evangelism and apologetic arguments for the faith and long-form conversations with solid faith leaders about relevant aspects of Christian doctrine.
- *Training Digital Evangelists.* Equip believers to be bold online witnesses. Digital evangelists should be trained to engage respectfully and thoughtfully with those caught up in the rising tide of Pagan ideologies. By using the tools of the digital age, Christians can confront false beliefs, answer questions, and invite people into the truth of the Gospel.
- *Look to the Next Thing.* As technology continues to evolve at an exponential rate, Christians must look ahead to the next platform, app, or form of media that will shape public discourse. Today, it's social media; tomorrow, it could be virtual reality, AI-driven content, or something entirely new. Just as the church adapted to the printing press and the invention of radio, television, and podcasts,

we must stay ahead of the curve and strategically leverage emerging technologies for the advancement of the Gospel. This means investing in understanding these platforms, whether it's TikTok, new streaming services, or decentralized web applications, and figuring out how to utilize them to reach people where they are. By pioneering the next wave of Christian content, we ensure that our message isn't merely reactive, but proactively engaging with the culture on the cutting edge.

4. Redouble Efforts to Reach Today's Youth

As we've discussed, young people are being influenced by alternative spiritualities and secular ideologies at an unprecedented rate, especially through social media. We must redouble our efforts to reach this generation before they are fully swept into the current of deception. Here are a few ideas:

- *Invest in Youth Ministry.* It's critical to make youth ministry (K-12) a priority by building programs that equip young people with solid biblical teaching and engaging them in active discipleship. We need to make Christianity relevant and compelling, addressing the challenges that youth face today, including the pressure to conform to worldly values.
- *Mentorship and Role Models.* We need older Christians—both parents and church leaders—to take a more active role in mentoring the youth, showing them how to navigate a world that increasingly embraces Paganism and secularism. Mentorship is essential in helping young believers hold fast to their faith.

- *Go Where They Are.* Reaching today's youth requires a dual approach: Engaging digitally and physically. The digital realm—social media, gaming platforms, and online communities—is where young people spend a significant portion of their time, shaping their ideas, opinions, and identities. To make an impact, the church must meet them there, using these platforms to deliver the Gospel in innovative and relevant ways. But we cannot stop at the screen. We must also be present in the physical spaces where young people gather—schools, sports fields, coffee shops, and local community events. We must build relationships in person, offering personal discipleship and guidance in their everyday lives.

5. Implement a Practical Strategy for Evangelism

Evangelism must become a direct and proactive part of the church's daily life. The traditional methods are no longer sufficient to reach the growing number of people influenced by secular ideologies and Pagan worldviews. For the church to make a significant impact, we must think outside the box and adopt new, innovative strategies. Here are three practical steps that can be implemented to enhance the church's evangelistic efforts and build stronger connections in a post-pandemic world.

- *New Attendee Onboarding System for Churches.* Evangelism doesn't stop at bringing people to church; it's about effectively integrating them into the life of the church. A well-designed onboarding system helps new attendees feel welcomed, valued and encouraged to take the next steps in their faith journey. This can include everything from personal follow-up communications to life group involvement and new member orientation classes. By making sure new people feel like they belong, we set the stage for lasting spiritual growth and deeper involvement in the life of the church.

- *Hybrid Evangelism.* Content creation provides a socially acceptable way to initiate evangelistic conversations. Street evangelism, which once felt awkward or intrusive, can now begin with simple introductions like, "Hi, I'm a content creator who makes videos about spiritual topics . . . would you mind if I asked you a few questions?" By bringing the Gospel to the streets—whether through filming evangelistic encounters, conducting interviews, or documenting community service—and sharing these experiences online, Christians can leverage this hybrid style of evangelism to reach a much larger audience than ever before. The key is to build genuine connections in person and then share those moments digitally, sparking wider conversations to impact lives around the world.

- *Recommit to Intentional Missions.* COVID-19 severely impacted mission work, limiting travel and disrupting outreach efforts. Now that the world is reopened, the church must recommit to intentional missions, both locally and globally. This means prioritizing both short-term and long-term, sustainable mission initiatives that focus on relationship-building, meeting tangible needs, and presenting the Gospel. And don't forget a camera. Mission trips offer a powerful opportunity for content creation—capturing authentic moments and sharing them online to raise awareness and amplify the Gospel message long after the trip ends. Another opportunity for hybrid evangelism, this blend of physical outreach and digital engagement can significantly expand the reach and impact of mission work.

6. Directly Combat False Doctrines and Pagan Ideologies

The onslaught of secularism, witchcraft, new-age philosophies, and other false beliefs is not just a cultural issue—it's a spiritual battle that demands both intellectual engagement and unwavering spiritual fortitude. As these deceptive ideologies infiltrate our culture, the church must actively engage with the world around us, boldly proclaiming biblical truth in the face of falsehoods. We are called to defend the faith, confront error head-on, and guide people back to the life-transforming power of the Gospel.[20] This requires a comprehensive approach—strengthening apologetics, exposing deceptive teachings, and re-engaging in fervent prayer for a world that desperately needs it.

- *Strengthen Apologetics.* Equip the church with the tools to defend the faith. Apologetics is not just for scholars like William Lane Craig, but for everyday believers who need to be able to articulate and defend the truth against the onslaught of false ideologies. This will require training in how to address specific issues like false doctrines, Pagan practices, Marxist ideology, and new sexual ethics.
- *Expose Deceptive Teachings.* The church must call out false teachings wherever they emerge—whether in the culture, popular media, or even within the church itself. Deceptive ideologies, such as New Thought and so-called "Christian witchcraft," that twist the Gospel or lead people into idolatry must be exposed and countered with biblical truth. However, believers must refrain from witch-hunts against fellow Christians over secondary differences. Disagreements on topics like spiritual gifts, head coverings, or women in ministry should not lead us to declare fellow brothers and sisters in Christ apostates. Instead, our focus must remain on confronting

truly heretical ideas that undermine the foundational doctrines of the faith—such as the nature of the Trinity, the divinity of Christ, salvation by grace through faith, or the sufficiency of Scripture. When we focus on these primary truths, we protect the integrity of the Gospel and maintain unity within the body of Christ.

- *Empower Prayer Warriors.* As we engage in defending the faith, we must also rely on the power of prayer. The church must raise up a new generation of prayer warriors who are committed to interceding for the body of Christ and the world around them. These prayer warriors will pray for wisdom in confronting false ideologies, for the protection of believers, and for the salvation of those trapped in deception. But be on guard—while intercession is a vital part of spiritual warfare, some forms of prayer may unknowingly cross a line by attempting to control or manipulate others, or by seeking to place ourselves in the position of God. For instance, intercession that disregards a person's free will or violates their personal agency can easily become spiritually harmful, even borderline witchcraft, despite being well-intentioned. We must remain grounded in the truth of Scripture and ensure our prayers align with God's will, not our own agendas. Through focused, persistent prayer, we invite the Holy Spirit to move powerfully in our hearts and in the hearts of others, always remembering that it is Christ who truly intercedes on our behalf before the Father.[21]

7. Renew Interest in Spiritual Gifts

One of the key takeaways throughout the pages of this book is that people have a deep, yet misguided, hunger for spiritual power.

Disillusioned with the emptiness of secular ideologies, many have turned to counterfeit sources of spiritual strength, oftentimes unknowingly, seeking fulfillment in demonic powers and mystical arts. While profoundly dangerous, it shows that people long for transcendence, supernatural experiences, and a sense of divine connection. But instead of turning to the true source of power—the Holy Spirit—they seek it in all the wrong places.

As we expand our evangelistic efforts, we must ensure that the American church is prepared to counter the powerful, yet false, spirituality promised by Paganism with a genuine and greater move of the Holy Spirit. It would be foolish to think that we could face the onslaught of counterfeit beliefs, the growing influence of Pagan ideologies, and the lust for demonic power armed with mere knowledge, strategies, or human effort. Only through the empowering presence of the Holy Spirit can we hope to engage effectively in this spiritual battle.

- *Teach on the Gifts of the Spirit.* Churches, across every denomination, should emphasize the significance of spiritual gifts and teach believers how to operate in them effectively and sober-mindedly. From prophecy to healing, from wisdom to discernment, these gifts are crucial for engaging with, and responding to, the spiritual needs of the culture around us. When we teach on the gifts, we invite believers into a deeper, more powerful relationship with the Holy Spirit and equip them to confront the darkness around them with God-given supernatural authority. The world is looking for answers, and the gifts of the Spirit provide the means to offer those answers in a way that transcends human ability.
- *Activate the Gifts.* Teaching alone is not enough. We must actively encourage and create spaces for believers

to step into the use of their spiritual gifts in everyday life. This requires a culture within the church where spiritual gifts are not just discussed but are actively cultivated, tested, and used. Whether it's prophesying over a hurting individual, praying for someone's healing, or discerning the truth amid deception, these gifts are weapons in the battle for souls. The Holy Spirit has equipped us for this moment in history, and it is only through His empowering that we will have the strength to combat the spiritual darkness and bring people to the truth of the Gospel.

A Word of Caution

As Paganism's influence grows in America, many Christians may become frustrated by the sluggish pace of the revivalistic work required to see cultural change. The effort of changing hearts and minds takes time, and for the overzealous, a temptation exists to accelerate the desired societal revival through more militant means. Once impatience sets in, it's easy to see force or coercion as the only available solution to push back the darkness to restore a spiritually righteous order in society. But history has shown the dangers of such approaches.

The Crusades, for example, which took place between the eleventh and fifteenth centuries, sought to impose Christian order through military conquest. Similarly, the Inquisition used legal and judicial measures, often including torture and execution, to suppress religious dissent within Christian communities, undermining religious liberty. These efforts, while rooted in religious zeal, ultimately threatened the very freedoms they sought to protect and created division rather than unity. In fact, despite taking place hundreds of years ago, many unbelievers still cite these events among the reasons why they reject the Christian faith.

However, we must remember that there is a better way—one that seeks, without violating an individual's freedom of choice, to restore and affirm the essential truths found in the Gospel of Jesus Christ. Rather than giving in to the temptation of force, no matter how much we despise Pagan ideology, Christians are called to engage with the culture in a way that honors personal agency, extending the message of Christ through grace *and* truth, with the hope of bringing reconciliation to a fractured world. As Francis A. Schaeffer wisely warned:

> *In such circumstances, it seems that there are only two alternatives in the natural flow of events: first, imposes order or, second, our society once again affirming that base which gave freedom without chaos in the first place—God's revelation in the Bible and His revelation through Christ. We have seen . . . many of the implications of an imposed order. But rather than throwing up our hands and giving in, we should take seriously the second alternative.*[22]

As Schaeffer points out, we must choose between two alternatives: Imposed order or a return to the foundational truths that brought freedom without chaos. While the allure of imposed order may feel like a swift solution to the rising tide of Paganism, we must resist the temptation to repeat the mistakes of history. After the events of 2020, believers are not only aware, but many have personally experienced the consequences of totalitarian systems that use force to suppress freedom. Many of us saw firsthand how political power was wielded against our communities—churches were forced closed, worship practices were restricted, and, in many states, our right to gather in fellowship was limited—all in the name of control and safety.

Now that conservatives are in power, many Christians are rallying, and rightfully so, with righteous indignation, to ensure that these same tactics are not used against the church again in the future. We have experienced the oppressive weight of government overreach and the consequences of restrictions that infringed upon our God-given fundamental rights.

However, in our righteous indignation and desire to protect our freedoms against godless ideologies, we must heed Schaeffer's counsel and resist the temptation to adopt the same coercive tactics we have fought against. While it is crucial to oppose the corrupt ideologies and Pagan movements that threaten our values, we must remember that our response should be rooted in the principles of grace and truth, not in the use of force or control. As we seek to safeguard our liberties, we must navigate the delicate tension between honoring the dignity and freedom of every individual, while simultaneously ensuring that evil does not gain a foothold in our society. This balance is, of course, much easier said than done.

The right road forward involves increasing religious freedoms, extending favor to churches and Christian organizations, and platforming Christian voices that will encourage faith to flourish—without resorting to the outright banning of Pagan practices or suppressing other belief systems, assuming they don't present an immediate danger to individuals or society. By choosing this path, we reject the temptation to impose a forced façade of righteousness—one that grants only the appearance of morality but fails to genuinely transform the hearts of individuals within the nation we seek to protect. True change comes not from external coercion, but from internal transformation, which is only possible through the freedom to choose, the grace of God, and the power of the Gospel. This is the road that leads to lasting peace and reconciliation rooted in true righteousness rather than superficial conformity.

Such actions prove that the appeal of Christianity lies not in political persuasion or military might but in its superior logic and the greater Gospel it offers. Christianity's transformative power is not found in coercion or force, but in its compelling message that God "has reconciled us to Himself through Christ."[23] The Gospel can change hearts and minds through the love of Christ, which offers a lasting and genuine solution to the world's brokenness—something Paganism could never provide. As G.K. Chesterton writes:

> It is said that Paganism is a religion of joy and Christianity of sorrow; it would be just as easy to prove that Paganism is pure sorrow and Christianity pure joy. Such conflicts mean nothing and lead nowhere. Everything human must have in it both joy and sorrow; the only matter of interest is the manner in which the two things are balanced or divided. And the really interesting thing is this, that the Pagan was happier and happier as he approached the earth, but sadder and sadder as he approached the heavens.[24]

Paganism, as Chesterton reminds us, in its pursuit of earthly pleasure, can never offer the fullness of joy that Christianity provides. While both Christians and Pagans might endure both earthly joy and sorrow, only the Gospel of Jesus Christ offers the lasting hope of reconciliation with God and eternal life. Hopefully, by now it's clear that the difference between these worldviews is not just in their outward practices, but in the essence of what they place their hope in. Paganism's idols—whether wealth, pleasure, or power—are empty, incapable of offering anything more than temporary satisfaction. This is not a new observation. In fact, the Bible has been warning us about the futility of idols for thousands of years.

In Psalm 115:4-8 CSB we read:

Their idols are silver and gold, made by human hands. They have mouths, but cannot speak; eyes, but cannot see. They have ears, but cannot hear; noses, but cannot smell. They have hands, but cannot feel; feet, but cannot walk; they cannot make a sound with their throats. Those who make them are just like them, as are all who trust in them.

These empty idols—whether they manifest as witchcraft, self-worship, or the hollow promises of power—are powerless to bring lasting change. They stand mute, blind, and impotent, offering only the illusion of fulfillment. Christianity, on the other hand, is grounded in the living God who speaks, who hears, and who acts. The God of the Bible is not distant; He is a personal God who entered human history through Jesus Christ to offer salvific redemption to all who would believe. His Gospel is alive and active, capable of restoring hearts and renewing lives in a way that Paganism can never match.

To win the battle against Paganism, we must do more than merely resist the rise of its idols; we must believe in Christianity in a way that shapes our lives, our actions, and our very hearts. It is not enough to claim the name of Christ or to oppose the darkness with moral outrage; we must embrace the light, letting it pierce the deepest corners of our souls. The world does not need a Christianity of convenience or cultural compliance; it needs a Christianity that is fervent, passionate, and unapologetically true. For only when we believe, with all our hearts, that Christ is the way, the truth, and the life—only when we are convinced that the Gospel is not just a set of doctrines but the living, breathing power of God—will we have the courage to stand against the forces of Paganism. And in doing so, we will not only win the battle, but we will see the world, broken and lost, healed and restored by the love and truth of Christ. For this is the victory we are promised, a victory that is "not by strength or by might,"[25] but by the power of God. May this serve as our reminder that the Christian has no need to cower in the corner at the shadow of evil, for he knows something the devil dare not admit: his defeat is not merely certain—it is already written. And in the end, it is not Hell that has the last word, but Heaven that has the final joy.

Notes

Chapter One

1. From the ancient Greek for sorcery. https://theomagica.com/goeteia.
2. https://www.instagram.com/chthoniclesbian?igsh=MXdwYWgza GZoM3M1dA==.
3. https://www.nbcnews.com/think/opinion/paganism-witchcraft-are -making-comeback-rcna54444.
4. https://www.urbandictionary.com/define.php?term=Harry%20 Potter%20Generation.
5. https://seattlespectator.com/2021/04/28/the-so-called-school -shooting-generation/.
6. https://mccrindle.com.au/article/topic/generation-z/the-substantial -impact-covid-19-has-had-on-gen-z/.
7. https://outschool.com/online-classes/age-groups/teenagers-witches.
8. https://wiccaacademy.com/video-courses/.
9. https://wiccaacademy.com/.
10. https://www.learnreligions.com/celebrity-pagans-and-wiccans -2561438.
11. Ibid.
12. For instance, in *Chilling Adventures of Sabrina*, the protagonist, Sabrina, challenges traditional gender roles and patriarchal structures within the witch community, advocating for equality and autonomy. Additionally, the series features diverse characters and relationships, including LGBTQ+ representation.
13. 2 Corinthians 10:4-5 CSB.
14. http://www.thelemapedia.org/index.php/Holy_Guardian_Angel.
15. https://latin-dictionary.net/definition/28482/occultus-occulta#:~ :text=Definitions%3A,%5Bin%20occulto%20%3D%3E%20secretly %5D.

16. https://www.theosophical.org/component/content/article?id=1040.
17. *Pagan America*, John Daniel Davidson, Regnery, pg. xiv.
18. *Pagan America*, pg. xv.
19. abortion-is-sacred-and-the-supreme-court-cant-take-that-away
     -from-us.
20. https://pluralism.org/sacred-bodies.
21. *The Christian Left*, Lucas Miles, Broadstreet Publishing Group, LLC,
     pg. 17.
22. https://www.counterpunch.org/2012/11/27/to-appease-the-gods
     -human-sacrifices-must-be-offered/.
23. https://www.learnreligions.com/pagans-and-polyamory-2561724.
24. *Queering Your Craft*, Cassandra Snow, Weiser Books, page xvii.
25. http://cassandra-snow.com/.
26. *Queering Your Craft*, pg. xxii.
27. Ibid., pg. xxii.
28. Ibid., pg. 220.
29. Ibid., pg. 220.
30. Ibid., pg. 191.
31. Ibid., pg. 226.
32. Ibid., pg. 165.
33. Ibid., pg. 146.
34. Ibid., pg. 143.
35. Ibid., pg. 228.
36. *The Marxification of Education*, James Lindsay, Kindle, pg. 8.
37. Ibid., pg. 8.
38. Ibid., pg. 8.
39. Ibid., pg. 8.
40. Ibid., pg. 42.
41. *Pedagogy of the Oppressed*, Paulo Freire, Continuum Publishing
     Company, pg. 100.
42. *Queering Your Craft*, pg. xxii.
43. 1 Peter 3:15 CSB.
44. *The End of Faith*, Sam Harris, pg. 85.
45. https://ehrmanblog.org/did-christians-invent-hospitals/.
46. https://www.humancoalition.org/impact/blog/debunking-five
     -common-pro-abortion-claims/.
47. https://www.seesharppress.com/20reasons.html#numberone.
48. John 15:18-21a CSB.
49. Matthew 8:29 CSB.

Chapter Two

1.   https://www.youtube.com/watch?v=OLSWVCwy88g.

2. Ibid.
3. https://www.animationmagazine.net/2024/01/vivienne-medranos
    -hazbin-hotel-scores-top-global-animation-debut-on-prime-video/#.
4. As described on the Amazon Prime app description of the show.
5. *Hazbin Hotel*, episode 1.
6. https://jwa.org/node/23210, Alphabet of Ben Sira 78: Lilith.
7. https://jwa.org/encyclopedia/article/lilith#pid-13701.
8. Isaiah 34:14 AMP.
9. *Demons*, Dr. Michael Heiser, Lexham Press 2020, pg. 29.
10. https://ia803000.us.archive.org/21/items/BabySnatchingDemons
    RestlessSoulsAndSTAMPATO/Baby_Snatching_Demons_Restless_
    Souls_and%20STAMPATO.pdf.
11. *Satanic Feminism*, Per Faxneld, Oxford University Press, pg. 2.
12. *Occult Feminism*, Rachel Wilson, pg. 9.
13. *The Women's Bible*, Elizabeth Cady Stanton, Kindle, pg. 230.
14. Ibid., pg. 5.
15. *Occult Feminism*, pg. 55.
16. Ibid., pg. 55.
17. Ibid., pgs. 56–57.
18. *The Women's Bible*, Stanton, Kindle Version, pg. 11.
19. Ibid., pg. 10.
20. Ibid., pgs. 10–11.
21. Ibid., pg. 11.
22. Ibid., pg. 7.
23. Ibid., pg. 7.
24. Ibid., pg. 7.
25. *Occult Feminism*, pg. 60.
26. *Satanic Feminism*, pg. 127.
27. *Occult Feminism*, pg. 61.
28. *Satanic Feminism*, pg. 53.
29. Ibid., pg. 111.
30. *Isis Unveiled*, Helena Blavatsky, Kindle, pg. 133.
31. *Satanic Feminism*, pg. 113.
32. *The Secret Doctrine*, Volume II, H.P. Blavatsky, pg. 318.
33. Ibid., pg. 319.
34. https://www.theosophical.org/publications/quest-magazine/
    wise-men-from-the-east-the-myth-of-the-hierarchy-of-adepts.
35. *Isis Unveiled*, pg. 10.
36. Ibid., pg. 341.
37. Ibid., pg. 385.
38. Ibid., pg. 386.
39. Ibid., pg. 311.
40. https://www.beyoncemass.com/.

41. https://www.youtube.com/watch?v=PXci-sRayAQ&t=33s.
42. https://www.beyoncemass.com/.
43. https://national-church-of-bey.tumblr.com/.
44. https://www.deseret.com/2014/5/23/20541999/is-the-church-dedicated-to-beyonce-just-a-joke/.
45. https://x.com/Playboy/status/830959071566012416.
46. https://x.com/crdanexo/status/1552878809329844224.
47. https://x.com/beyoncesdealer/status/1069326045814423562.
48. https://time.com/4306316/beyonce-lemonade-black-woman-magic/.
49. https://www.foxnews.com/media/taylor-swift-themed-church-service-attract-1000-worshippers.
50. https://www.foxnews.com/media/where-does-taylor-swift-stand-issues-political-history-pop-superstar.
51. https://www.christianpost.com/news/taylor-swifts-new-album-mocks-god-christians-critics-say.html.
52. Ibid.
53. https://www.foxnews.com/media/where-does-taylor-swift-stand-issues-political-history-pop-superstar.
54. https://x.com/Yolo304741/status/1756861740959006990.
55. https://www.foxnews.com/entertainment/pop-artists-turning-to-satanic-imagery-to-drum-up-controversy-sales-experts-say.
56. https://www.tiktok.com/@whoiisonika/video/7242022150125702427.
57. https://pagesix.com/2025/02/02/style/bianca-censori-hits-grammys-2025-carpet-in-bare-stocking-dress-with-kanye-west/.
58. *Defending Pornography*, Nadine Strossen, NYU Press, Kindle, location 4123.
59. Ibid., location 4512.
60. *Pagan America*, pg. 35.
61. https://medium.com/@Agency-Onlyfans/top-10-highest-earning-onlyfans-creators-and-their-monthly-income-in-2024-62f182c97685.
62. https://www.enterpriseappstoday.com/stats/onlyfans-stats.html.
63. https://usechatterly.com/blog-full/how-many-creators-are-there-on-only-fans.
64. https://www.knowledgeformen.com/how-onlyfans-affects-womens-lives-relationships-social-value-future-opportunities/#:~:text=Many%20women%20start%20out%20on,channels%20with%20slightly%20better%20angles.
65. Ibid.
66. Proverbs 5:4-5 CSB.
67. https://www.tiktok.com/t/ZPRE9XnJM/.
68. *The Sacrament of Abortion*, Ginette Paris, Spring Publications, pg. 107.
69. Ibid.

70. Ibidl, pg. 92.
71. *The Complete Works of Margaret Sanger*, Margaret Sanger, Shrine of Knowledge, Kindle, pg. 291.
72. Ibid., pg. 291.
73. Ibid., pg. 288.
74. Ibid., pg. 288.
75. https://awpc.cattcenter.iastate.edu/directory/margaret-h-sanger/# :~:text=She%20joined%20the%20Socialist%20Party,the%20basic %20cause%20of%20poverty.
76. *Occult Feminism*, pgs. 94–95.
77. John 3:16 CSB.
78. Ibid.

Chapter Three

1. https://www.irishtimes.com/culture/god-make-way-for-gaia-a -deity-even-atheists-can-believe-in-1.4265949.
2. Ibid.
3. Ibid.
4. *Occult Feminism*, pg. 103.
5. https://www.usccb.org/committees/pro-life-activities/myth -overpopulation-and-folks-who-brought-it-you.
6. Ibid.
7. Ibid.
8. https://www.ncbi.nlm.nih.gov/search/research-news/17030/#:~: text=Billionaire%20Elon%20Musk%20tweeted%2C%20not,it's%20 difficult%20to%20compare%20problems.
9. *Superabundance*, Marian Tupy and Gale L. Pooley, Cato Institute, Kindle, pg. 502.
10. Ibid., pgs. 502–503.
11. https://www.usatoday.com/story/news/politics/onpolitics/2019/ 01/22/ocasio-cortez-climate-change-alarm/2642481002/.
12. https://medium.com/@poetsarah/greta-for-gaia-d8488b15dc23.
13. https://www.theguardian.com/commentisfree/2021/nov/02/beware -gaia-theory-climate-crisis-earth.
14. *Gaia: A New Look at Life on Earth*, James Lovelock, Oxford University Press, Kindle, location 99.
15. https://www.blueletterbible.org/lexicon/g5331/kjv/tr/0-1/.
16. Ibid.
17. https://www.statista.com/statistics/1202065/population-with-covid -vaccine-by-state-us/.
18. https://www.thecut.com/2021/09/covid-pandemic-isolation -witchcraft.html.

19. Ibid.
20. Ibid.
21. https://www.biblegateway.com/passage/?search=Romans%201%3A 28&version=CSB.
22. https://www.facebook.com/share/p/1FQ3icobYV/?mibextid=wwXIfr.
23. https://www.gotquestions.org/pagan-paganism.html.
24. https://www.youtube.com/watch?v=Ru8i5r-un8U.
25. https://www.tiktok.com/@arianagrande/video/7237906839952723246 ?embed_source=121374463%2C121442748%2C121439635%2C121 433650%2C121404359%2C121351166%2C121331973%2C1208115 92%2C120810756%3Bnull%3Bembed_pause_share&refer=embed& referer_url=www.billboard.com%2Fculture%2Fproduct. -recommendations%2Fbest-tarot-decks-beginner-friendly-celebrity -approved-1235342351%2F%23&referer_video_id=7237906839952 723246.
26. https://www.youtube.com/watch?v=kHLHSlExFis.
27. https://www.tabletmag.com/sections/news/articles/ariana-grande -credits-kabbalah-for-her-success.
28. Ibid.
29. https://www.newsweek.com/britney-spears-religions-instagram -baptist-kabbalah-1524875.
30. https://www.latimes.com/archives/la-xpm-2004-sep-24-oe-halevi24 -story.html.
31. https://abcnews.go.com/Entertainment/demi-moore-ashton -kutcher-kabbalah-crutch/story?id=14707122#:~:text=Moore%20 and%20Kutcher%20have%20been,weekend%20with%20a%20 Kabbalah%20leader.
32. https://pagesix.com/2014/09/04/gwyneth-paltrow-is-becoming-an -actual-jewish-princess/.
33. https://abcnews.go.com/2020/story?id=855125&page=1.
34. https://www.marieclaire.com/beauty/doing-well-vanessa-hudgens/.
35. https://www.facebook.com/reel/157006640357030.
36. Romans 1:25 CSB.
37. https://www.dailymail.co.uk/sciencetech/article-13105301/anna -paulina-luna-believes-UFOs-not-human-origin.html.
38. https://www.washingtonpost.com/national-security/2024/03/08/ no-ufo-aliens-pentagon-report/.
39. https://www.space.com/climate-change-message-to-aliens.
40. Ibid.
41. *There Were Giants Upon the Earth*, Zecharia Sitchin, Bear & Company, Kindle, pg. 344.
42. https://www.bostonglobe.com/2024/03/27/opinion/new-religion -americans-ufos-aliens/.

43. Ibid.
44. Genesis 6:1-4 CSB.
45. *Apocalypse: A Spiritual Guide to the Second Coming*, Dr. Jim Richards, True Potential, Inc., Kindle, pg. 44.
46. https://www.artnews.com/art-in-america/aia-reviews/i-want-to -believe-gittlitz-posadism-ufos-apocalypse-communism-1202692978/.
47. https://www.thenation.com/article/society/aliens-socialism -posadism-ufos/.
48. https://www.astronomy.com/science/these-are-the-ways-our-world -will-end/.
49. https://www.itmustbenow.com/feature/our-big-questions/8-things -killing-planet/.
50. In Norse mythology, Ragnarok is an apocalyptic event leading to the destruction of the cosmos and the death of the gods.
51. https://www.shamansmarket.com/blogs/musings/is-this-the-end -of-days-the-prophecy-of-the-eagle-and-the-condor.
52. Revelation 21:1 CSB.
53. https://www.pbs.org/newshour/politics/court-upholds-californias -authority-to-set-nation-leading-vehicle-emission-rules.
54. https://www.cnn.com/2023/05/03/us/new-york-natural-gas-ban -climate/index.html.
55. https://www.foxnews.com/politics/united-nations-set-call -americans-reduce-meat-consumption.
56. https://www.foxbusiness.com/economy/world-economic-forum -calls-reduce-private-vehicles-by-eliminating-ownership.
57. https://medium.com/betterism/yin-yang-holds-a-secret-for-inner -and-global-peace-c5177bd2cfa1.
58. 1 John 1:5-7 CSB.

Chapter Four

1. https://nypost.com/2023/06/28/new-study-on-rise-in-transgender -shows-its-a-fad-especially-among-young-girls/.
2. Ibid.
3. https://www.usatoday.com/story/opinion/voices/2019/02/11/ transgender-debate-transitioning-sex-gender-column/1894076002/.
4. https://www.npr.org/sections/shots-health-news/2025/01/06/nx-s1 -5247724/transgender-teens-gender-affirming-care-hormones-jama.
5. https://www.usatoday.com/story/news/health/2023/08/23/gender -affirming-care-restrictions-for-minors-grow/70652104007/.
6. https://www.forbes.com/sites/joshuacohen/2023/06/06/increasing -number-of-european-nations-adopt-a-more-cautious-approach-to -gender-affirming-care-among-minors/.

7. https://www.bbc.com/news/world-europe-66200194.
8. https://acpeds.org/transgender-interventions-harm-children.
9. https://www.hrc.org/resources/get-the-facts-on-gender-affirming-care
10. https://www.reuters.com/article/world/pope-says-gender-theory.
    -part-of-global-war-on-marriage-family-idUSKCN1213KG/.
11. https://www.samhsa.gov/grants/grants-dashboard?f%5B0%5D=by_
    nofo_number%3AFG-23-004#awards-tab.
12. https://www.whitehouse.gov/briefing-room/statements-releases/
    2023/12/11/fact-sheet-the-united-states-response-to-ugandas-anti
    -homosexuality-act-and-persistent-human-rights-abuses/.
13. *Pagan America*, pgs. 207–208.
14. Ibid., pg. 208.
15. Ibid., pg. 209.
16. https://www.dailymail.co.uk/sport/olympics/article-13677879/An
    -Olympic-balls-Eagle-eyed-viewers-spot-performers-TESTICLE
    -hanging-opening-ceremony-Paris-2024-dancer-suffers-x-rated
    -wardrobe-malfunction.html.
17. https://en.wikipedia.org/wiki/Motte-and-bailey_fallacy.
18. https://www.forbes.com/sites/soniathompson/2024/07/29/was-an
    -apology-necessary-from-paris-olympics-for-opening-ceremony/.
19. https://www.politico.com/news/2022/03/22/blackburn-jackson
    -define-the-word-woman-00019543.
20. *Lucifer*, 1890 October, https://theosophy.world/sites/default/files/
    Theosophical%20Publications/Lucifer/1890/lucifer_v7_n38_
    october_1890.pdf.
21. *Summa Theologia*, Aquinas, Book 1, Q. 50, Art. 2, Kindle, location
    9754.
22. https://www.britannica.com/topic/Baphomet
23. Ibid.
24. *Satanic Feminism*, pgs. 53–54.
25. Ibid., pg. 53.
26. Ibid., pg. 53.
27. Ibid., pg. 46.
28. Ibid., pg. 46.
29. Ibid., pg. 47.
30. Ibid., pgs. 47–48.
31. *The Secret History of Hermes Trismegistus*, Florian Ebeling, Cornell
    University Press, Kindle, pg 9.
32. Mercury is the Roman equivalent of the Greek Hermes.
33. *The Secret History of Hermes Trismegistus*, pg. 5.
34. Ibid., location 36.
35. *Saint Augustine of Hippo: The City of God*, St. Augustine, Kindle,
    Location 9825.

36. https://youtu.be/SH0D69_ti-Y?si=t3Kkbe8S_8p4mEBf.
37. https://youtu.be/SH0D69_ti-Y?si=vxzzWeM93dCTNyTq.
38. *The Emerald Tablet of Hermes & The Kybalion*, Hermes Trismegistus & The Three Initiates, Mockingbird Press, pg. 5.
39. Ibid., pg. 74.
40. https://remitchelljr.com/2016/07/15/youre-a-hermeticist-whats-that/.
41. https://www.christianpost.com/news/parents-who-lost-custody-of-child-ask-supreme-court-to-hear-case.html.
42. https://www.iwf.org/identity-crisis-stories/jeannette-cooper/.
43. *The Emerald Tablet of Hermes & The Kybalion*, pg. 103.
44. *The Corpus Hermeticum*, Hermes Trismegistus, Majestic, pg. 50.
45. Ibid., pg. 51.
46. Ibid., pg. 50.
47. Ibid., pg. 6.
48. Ibid., pg. 50.
49. Ibid., pg. 73.
50. https://www.theguardian.com/education/2004/apr/01/research.highereducation.
51. Ibid.
52. Ibid.
53. https://thefederalist.com/2021/12/06/vaccine-segregation-and-quarantine-camps-are-flashing-warnings-to-stop-covid-insanity-before-its-too-late/.
54. https://www.politico.com/news/2024/06/02/fauci-covid-research-investigative-panel-00161109.
55. https://www.politico.com/news/2023/08/03/sun-shield-earth-asteroid-00109104.

Chapter Five

1. https://x.com/iamlisalogan/status/1783479858347331738.
2. https://www.evolutionaryleaders.net/.
3. https://x.com/iamlisalogan/status/1783479870049423703.
4. https://www.evolutionaryleaders.net/acalltoconsciousevolution/the-call.
5. https://sdgthoughtleaderscircle.org/about/.
6. https://www.thepositiveencourager.global/robert-mullers-work-to-build-a-positive-planet/.
7. http://www.goodmorningworld.org/paradiseplan/, Idea 4515.
8. Ibid., Idea 4886.
9. *The Seicus Circle: A Humanist Revolution*, Claire Chambers, pg. 5.
10. *The Naked Communist*, W. Cleon Skousen, Kindle, pg. 273.
11. Ibid., pg. 274.
12. *Apocalypse*, pgs. 148–149.

13. Ibid., p. 150.
14. https://www.carolinajournal.com/opinion/what-can-be-unburdened
     -by-what-has-been/.
15. https://x.com/ConceptualJames/status/1819391183753277631.
16. https://www.washingtonexaminer.com/news/business/3130495/
     socialists-mad-harris-giving-them-what-they-thought-they-wanted/
     ?utm_source=google&utm_medium=cpc&utm_campaign=Pmax_
     USA_Magazine_21-June-Intent-Audience-Signals&gad_source
     =1&gbraid=0AAAAAD8dCuyiOClRxgPQ5VrGiCbjdJ6OK&gclid
     =Cj0KCQjw8--2BhCHARIsAF_w1gxnIMCZfqLf_WmTOOUZGp
     Emnpx-PiN85IdtIBzDD9LNWeP78Xrigy0aAvPFEALw_wcB.
17. https://www.wired.com/1995/07/technopagans/.
18. https://x.com/mpesce.
19. https://www.wired.com/1995/07/technopagans/.
20. Ibid.
21. Ibid.
22. Ibid.
23. Ibid.
24. 2 Thessalonians 2:4 CSB.
25. *The Naked Communist*, pg. 283.
26. Ibid.
27. Ibid.
28. Ibid., pg. 280.
29. Donald Trump first debated Joe Biden, and then later debated
     Kamala Harris.
30. https://timesofindia.indiatimes.com/world/us/who-is-donald-harris
     -academic-behind-trumps-marxist-claims-against-kamala/articleshow/
     113248637.cms.
31. https://nypost.com/2023/07/07/teens-says-tiktok-influenced-her-to
     -identify-as-transgender/.
32. *The Great Narrative*, Klaus Schwab and Thierry Malleret, World
     Economic Forum, pg. 185.
33. https://x.com/FiveTimesAugust/status/1520031926882652162?ref_
     src=twsrc%5Etfw%7Ctwcamp%5Etweetembed%7Ctwterm%5E152
     0031926882652162%7Ctwgr%5E6e6328960f02d119dace88411223
     c96b3df6f5ec%7Ctwcon%5Es1_c10&ref_url=https%3A%2F%2F
     www.redditmedia.com%2Fmediaembed%2F1032vww%2F%3F
     responsive%3Dtrueis_nightmode%3Dfalse.
34. https://www.youtube.com/watch?v=YhwJH1fncv8.

Chapter Six

1. https://www.youtube.com/watch?v=wlO3KJWnNd8.
2. Deuteronomy 18:10-12 CSB.

3. https://www.youtube.com/watch?v=wlO3KJWnNd8.
4. *Gurdjieff and the Fourth Way,* Stephen A. Grant, Shambhala Publications, Kindle, pg. 13.
5. Ibid., pg. 3.
6. Ibid., pg. 283.
7. Ibid., pg. 13.
8. Ibid., pg. 283.
9. Ibid., pg. 289.
10. 2 Corinthians 6:14-15.
11. https://www.blueletterbible.org/lexicon/g955/kjv/tr/0-1/.
12. Ibid.
13. 2 Corinthians 11:3-4 CSB.
14. https://www.pewresearch.org/short-reads/2018/01/22/american-religious-groups-vary-widely-in-their-views-of-abortion/.
15. *Prescription Against Heretics,* Tertullian, Beloved Publishing LLC, Kindle, location 115.
16. *New Days, Old Demons: Ancient Paganism Masquerading as Progressive Christianity,* Mark Driscoll, RealFaith, Kindle, pg. 60.
17. https://www.pewresearch.org/religious-landscape-study/database/christians/christian/views-about-homosexuality/.
18. 1 Samuel 15:23 CSB.
19. 1 Kings 14:23-24 CSB.
20. https://www.theoi.com/Olympios/Dionysos.html.
21. *The Descent of Ishtar,* Timothy J. Stephany, Kindle, 2015.
22. https://www.theoi.com/Olympios/Dionysos.html.
23. 1 Kings 11:1-6 CSB.

Chapter Seven

1. *Strange New World,* Carl R. Trueman, Crossway, pg. 174.
2. https://christiancitizen.us/is-american-christianity-oppressive/.
3. *The God Delusion,* Richard Dawkins, Tantor Audio, pg. 259.
4. https://x.com/thegreatODEN1/status/1662782034878578688.
5. https://x.com/StefCvetkovic/status/1780860690086908373.
6. https://www.nbcnews.com/think/opinion/racism-among-white-christians-higher-among-nonreligious-s-no-coincidence-ncna1235045.
7. *Strange New World,* pg. 174.
8. Ibid.
9. Ibid.
10. For more on this, I'd recommend reading my book, *Woke Jesus: The False Messiah Destroying Christianity.*
11. *Strange New World,* pg. 101.

12. Ibid.
13. Genesis 3:1 CSB.
14. Exodus 16:2-3 CSB.
15. Job 42:7 CSB.
16. Genesis 3:5 CSB.
17. For those looking for more on this subject, I explore it in depth in my first book, *Good God: The One We Want to Believe In but Are Afraid to Embrace.*
18. *The God Delusion*, pg. 251.
19. Ibid.
20. Ibid.
21. Ibid.
22. www.instagram.com/christopherhitchens.
23. *God Is Not Great: How Religion Poisons Everything*, Christopher Hitchens, Hachette Audio, Kindle, location 208.
24. https://x.com/Lilith_Atheist/status/1856069552448122889.
25. *God Is Not Great*, pg. 16.
26. Ibid.
27. *The God Delusion*, pgs. 289–290.
28. Ibid.
29. Acts 4:12 CSB.
30. https://medium.com/inspire-believe-grow/the-sexist-writings-of-st-paul-2526c957751b.
31. *Strange New World*, pg. 174.
32. *First and Second Apologies*, Justin Martyr, Beloved Publishing LLC, pgs. 2–3.
33. Ibid., pg. 4.
34. Ibid., pg. 8.
35. Ibid.. pg 55.
36. Ibid., pg. 5.
37. Ibid., pg. 6.
38. Ibid., pg. 2.
39. Ibid., pg. 8.
40. *Strange New World*, pgs. 176–177.
41. Ibid., p. 176.

Chapter Eight

1. Acts 26:29 CSB.
2. *Reasonable Faith*, Third Edition, William Lane Craig, Two Words Publishing, LLC, pg. 18.
3. https://www.wsj.com/business/media/sales-of-bibles-are-booming-fueled-by-first-time-buyers-and-new-versions-d402460e#.

4. https://cbn.com/news/us/bible-sales-are-skyrocketing-whats-going.
5. Ibid.
6. https://www.spectator.co.uk/article/the-unlikely-christian
   -conversion-of-russell-brand/.
7. https://people.com/charlie-sheen-and-denise-richards-daughter
   -lola-got-baptized-after-feeling-lost-and-hopeless-8779082.
8. https://apnews.com/article/shia-lebeouf-actor-catholic-church
   -conversion-47cc67b06d9ce3f436c745f0fafl a84f.
9. https://www.hollywoodreporter.com/news/general-news/denzel
   -washington-becomes-minister-1236093019/.
10. https://www.asbury.edu/about/revival-history/outpouring/.
11. https://chvnradio.com/articles/god-lit-a-match-baptize-california
    -saw-12000-baptized-in-2-days.
12. https://cbn.com/news/entertainment/something-incredible
    -happening-multiple-college-football-players-point-jesus.
13. https://www.bbc.com/culture/article/20240209-couple-to-throuple
    -how-polyamory-is-becoming-a-new-normal.
14. https://thehill.com/homenews/house/501633-pelosi-schumer
    -kneel-in-silence-for-almost-9-minutes-to-honor-george-floyd/.
15. https://www.npr.org/2024/08/16/nx-s1-5058669/abortion-democrats
    -chicago-dnc-illinois-reproductive-rights-roe.
16. Romans 1:19-20 CSB.
17. Isaiah 55:7 CSB.
18. 1 Corinthians 10:4-5 CSB.
19. Romans 2:24 CSB.
20. James 1:13 CSB.
21. Isaiah 55:9 CSB.
22. Isaiah 55:7 CSB.
23. Isaiah 55:8 CSB.
24. 1 John 4:8 CSB.
25. John 8:36 CSB.
26. 1 Corinthians 12:12 CSB.
27. John 11:25 CSB.
28. Colossians 1:16 CSB.
29. Colossians 2:8 CSB.
30. 2 Peter 2:1 CSB.
31. Ibid., 2:3 CSB.
32. Ibid., 2:19 CSB.
33. https://onlinecoursesblog.hillsdale.edu/our-constitution-was-made
    -only-for-a-moral-and-religious-people/.
34. Romans 8:29 CSB.
35. Acts 17:22-31 CSB.

36. Acts 1:8 CSB.
37. 1 Thessalonians 1:5 CSB.

Chapter Nine

1. https://faithandleadership.com/more-pastors-age-and-retire-churches
-appear-be-facing-succession-crisis-study-says#:~:text=In%20
addition%2C%20the%20age%20of,2000%20to%2057%20in%20
2020.
2. https://www.truthnetwork.com/show/the-charlie-kirk-show-charlie
-kirk/92734/.
3. Matthew 25.
4. Ephesians 4:3 CSB.
5. *After Modernity—What?*, Thomas C. Oden, Zondervan, p. 165.
6. Ibid.
7. Ibid.
8. *Orthodoxy*, G.K. Chesterton, Hendrickson Publishers, p. 7.
9. The earliest variation was known as the Old Roman Creed.
10. https://www.learnreligions.com/the-apostles-creed-p2-700364.
11. *Treatise on Faith and the Creed*, St. Augustine, Lighthouse Publishing, Kindle, Location 79.
12. Ibid.
13. 1 Peter 1:3 CSB.
14. 1 John 4:13 CSB.
15. *How Should We Then Live?: The Rise and Decline of Western Thought and Culture*, Francis A. Schaeffer, Crossway, 2005, p. 256.
16. *Religionless Christianity*, Eric Metaxas, Blackstone Publishing, pg. vii.
17. *Strange New World*, p. 178.
18. *How Should We Then Live?*, p. 256.
19. Luke 19:13 KJV.
20. 1 Timothy 4:6 CSB.
21. Romans 8:34.
22. *How Should We Then Live?*, p. 252.
23. 2 Corinthians 5:18 CSB.
24. *Orthodoxy*, pg. 153–154.
25. Zechariah 4:6 CSB.

Acknowledgments

Writing *Pagan Threat* has been a journey of prayer, persistence, and partnership, and I'm incredibly grateful for the many people who stood with me along the way.

First, to my wife Krissy—your unwavering support, wisdom, and spiritual strength anchor everything I do. Thank you for believing in this message and in me, even through the long writing nights and busy travel days. To my church family at Nfluence Church, your prayers and encouragement continue to fuel the mission.

To Sarah, my brilliant editor, thank you for helping me sharpen every sentence while staying true to the vision. To Charlie Kirk, your boldness, vision, and steadfast defense of truth have helped shape a generation—I'm honored to serve alongside you in this battle for America's soul.

To the entire staff at TPUSA Faith, thank you for your tireless work and constant hustle in advancing the cause of righteousness in our time.

To Keith and the incredible team at Humanix Publishing, thank you for championing this book and giving it a national platform.

Matthew Faraci, your early introduction to Humanix and ongoing friendship made this project possible—thank you. Billy Hallowell, your regular check-ins and encouragement meant more than you know.

And to Cassandra and Asa, my executive assistants—thank you for keeping everything moving, managing the chaos, and helping make space for the words to flow. Your behind-the-scenes support gave me just enough breathing room to write this book among flights, sermons, and about a hundred speaking events.

Above all, I thank God, whose truth endures through every age and whose Word will outlast every idol.

Index

Orthodox Christianity:
Apostles' Creed in, 196
Hermetic beliefs and, 85–86
LGBTQ ideology and, 138–139
Pagan Christianity and, 141–142
syncretism and devolution of,
135–138
Wokeism in, 14–15
Outschool.com, 4

Pagan Christianity, xiii, 117–142
Enneagrams in, 118–121
LGBTQ ideology in, 138–141
Paul on, 121–122
pressure on orthodox
Christianity from, 141–142
spiritual/self-improvement
practices in, 122–133
and syncretism, 135–137
Paganism, xii
battle plan against, 206–218
combating ideologies of,
215–216
complacency about rise of,
191–194
criticisms of Christianity from,
145–147
defined, 5–6
Eclectic, 11
feminism and, 30
freedom promised by, 182–183
human longing underlying,
177–182
Justin's apology in face of,
159–162
Millennial and Gen Z converts
to, 3–5
morality and the sacred in, 11–16
postmodernism and, 147–148
secular, 9
strategies for countering,
xv–xvii

theosophist elites and spread
of, 93–94
transgenderism and, 72–75
types of, 6–11
and Woke ideology, xi–xii,
13–16
(See also Neo-Paganism; specific
types by name)
Pantheism, 181
Paris, Ginette, 44
Paul, Apostle, 121–122, 137, 165,
166, 168, 172, 178, 183,
186–187, 195
Pesce, Mark, 105–106
Peter, Apostle, 154, 184, 201
Philippians (Biblical book), 182
Pilate, Pontius, 199–200
Pilgrimages, 126–127
Plake, John, 167
Playboy, 35
Political engagement, 208–210
Pooley, Gale L., 51
Population growth, 49–53
Pornography, 39–42
Posadas, J., 63
Postmodernism, 147–149
Prayer warriors, 216
Presidential election (2024), 193
Primary Christian doctrine,
rooting discipleship in,
206–208
Proposition 139, Arizona, 192
Protestants, 133, 137, 202n
Proverbs (Biblical book), 41, 129,
130, 192–193
Psalms (Biblical book), 124, 180, 222
Public discourse, engaging in, 209

Quimby, Phineas, 10

Raztresen, Sara, 135
Reality, 107, 147

About the Author

LUCAS MILES is a trusted voice in the American church who has consistently addressed some of the most challenging topics in theology, politics, and culture. Lucas has been syndicated in articles across both political and religious news outlets, such as Newsmax, *The Blaze*, *FlashPoint*, Fox News, *The Washington Times*, CBN, and *The Christian Post*.

In addition to his latest books, *Pagan Threat: Confronting America's Godless Uprising* and *Woke Jesus: The False Messiah Destroying Christianity*, Lucas is the author of the bestselling book, *The Christian Left: How Liberal Thought Has Hijacked the Church*, and the critically acclaimed book, *Good God: The One We Want to Believe in But Are Afraid to Embrace*.

An ordained minister since 2004, Miles is the lead pastor of Nfluence Church in Granger, Indiana, the President of The Nfluence Network, and the Senior Director of TPUSA Faith serving under Charlie Kirk.

For booking requests and other resources, please visit LucasMiles.org.